LOADED

LOADED
Money, Psychology, and How to Get Ahead without Leaving Your Values Behind

Sarah Newcomb

WILEY

Published by John Wiley & Sons, Inc., Hoboken, New Jersey.
Published simultaneously in Canada.

For general information on our other products and services or for technical support, please contact our
Customer Care Department within the United States at (800) 762–2974, outside the United States at
(317) 572–3993 or fax (317) 572–4002.

Wiley publishes in a variety of print and electronic formats and by print-on-demand. Some material
included with standard print versions of this book may not be included in e-books or in print-on-
demand. If this book refers to media such as a CD or DVD that is not included in the version you
purchased, you may download this material at http://booksupport.wiley.com. For more information
about Wiley products, visit www.wiley.com.

Library of Congress Cataloging-in-Publication Data:

Names: Newcomb, Sarah C., author.
Title: Loaded : money, psychology, and how to get ahead without leaving your
   values behind / Sarah Newcomb, PhD.
Description: Hoboken, New Jersey : John Wiley & Sons, Inc., [2016] | Includes index.
Identifiers: LCCN 2016001707 | ISBN 9781119258322 (hardback) |
ISBN 9781119258339 (ePDF) | ISBN 9781119258346 (ePub)
Subjects: LCSH: Finance, Personal–Psychological aspects. |
   Economics–Psychological aspects. | BISAC: BUSINESS & ECONOMICS / Personal
   Finance / Money Management. | BUSINESS & ECONOMICS / Personal Finance /
   General. | BUSINESS & ECONOMICS / Personal Finance / Investing.
Classification: LCC HG179 .N447 2016 | DDC 332.024–dc23 LC record available at
http://lccn.loc.gov/2016001707

Printed in the United States of America
SKY10029331_082421

To Zoë: May you never stand in the way of your own dreams.

Contents

Acknowledgments

Thank you *to the following individuals, without whose contributions and support this book would not have been written:*

First, to the incredible professors who have inspired and challenged me, and taught me to diligently question my assumptions: Jim Grubman, George Criner, Mario Teisl, Shannon McCoy, Caroline Noblet, Bill Halteman, and Linda Silka. Your scholarship and support have made this work possible.

To my colleagues, who have championed and supported this work through many stages and drafts: Rob Pinkerton, Steve Wendel, Amna Kanoun, Merve Akbas, Erik Johnson, Mary Dyer, Marion Syverson, Ryan Pickering, Caroline Collins, Pedram Rahmatabati, Diane Batty, Renee Benz, Carling Spelhaug, and Michael Pettit. Your patience, creative contributions, encouragement, and cheerleading made all the difference in the world.

To the team at Wiley who believed in the idea and helped turn out a great work in record time: James Belcher, Michael Henton, Meg Freeborn, Susan Cerra, and especially Tula Batanchiev, who first saw the value in this work, and held my hand through the entire process. You all have been amazing.

To my family, and those friends that I love like family: Chris, Amy, Jesse, and Jake Newcomb; Jason Mills; Robin and Jim Hamilton; Zoë and Graham Morehead; Jonathan McCullum; Kristen Brown; Stacia Dreyer; and Michelle Johnson. If not for all you've given, this book would simply not exist.

Lastly, to all of the people who I have had the pleasure to teach and counsel over the years. Thank you for sharing your stories and your struggles. I am sure I learned far more from you than the other way around.

Introduction

THERE IS NO SHORTAGE of books for those who love money. Enter any bookstore and you will find guides to help you think rich, attract money, or beat Wall Street. These may appeal to people who aspire to great wealth and luxury and those who associate money with opportunity, happiness, and freedom. But where is the book for the rest of us? Where is the book for the people who have come to equate money with stress, inequality, barriers, or greed? Where is the book that acknowledges the darker side of the financial world?

That book is here.

My own journey into the world of financial psychology began in 2005 when, after receiving a bachelor's degree in mathematics, I still struggled to make sense of my financial life. As a summa cum laude in math, I had to admit that my issues with money had nothing to do with numbers. I love numbers. I had no trouble understanding interest rates and balance sheets. Why, then, wasn't I able to get a handle on my own money? Why did it seem that no matter how I tried, there was never enough?

In the fall of 2006, I began a graduate program in personal financial planning. I wanted to put an end to my financial stress, and learning how experts manage money seemed the most logical way. It was during my time at Bentley University that I met the teacher who would change my financial life and alter the course of my career. Dr. James Grubman's class, Psychology in Financial Planning, was a turning point. The purpose of the course was to prepare us as young financial planners for the client who would one day walk into our office feeling like a complete failure because he had only made $50 million that year.

How would we handle this? Would we inwardly scoff and judge, or would we listen long enough to understand that this young business owner lived in the shadow of his father's legacy, and that no matter how successful he became, he would remain convinced that his father could have done better?

I learned a priceless lesson from Dr. Grubman: A person's relationship with money is almost never about the numbers. It is about the stories we tell ourselves because of those numbers. Each of us has come to believe certain stories based on our upbringing and our experiences with money: stories about who we are and who we are not, stories about what we can and cannot do in the world. This is where our relationship with money is rooted, and this is where sound money management begins. It starts with a story.

When I examined my own relationship with money, I discovered that my story was filled with anger and resentment. Financial stress is survival stress, and by my mid-twenties I had scarcely known a day without it. As far back as I could remember, money had been a source of anxiety and conflict. My parents worked several jobs to keep food on the table for my three siblings and me. Unlike many, we never went hungry, and for that I am extremely grateful. Still, there was the tension, the anxiety, and the feeling of helplessness that accompanied daily life in a low-income family. As I grew to understand the world and my place within it, the dark cloud of lack seemed to hang over every part of life. Opportunities passed me by. Dreams were deferred, and deferred again, for lack of money. Social connections were hindered because I could not dress the part or afford the same hobbies and hangouts as my middle-class peers. By early adulthood I was worn down. I was poor. I always had been, and I always would be. It was as much a part of my identity as my name.

Many people respond to a childhood of lack by focusing all their energies on making as much money as possible in adulthood. I found this idea abhorrent. I had not only come to resent the lack of money but money itself. The culture of my immediate family, and many of the people I most respected, was anti-wealth. While I don't recall them saying it out loud, the message I absorbed from the people around me was clear: You either care about people, or you care about money. The logical extension of this belief is that people who focus on making a lot of money don't care about their fellows, but are driven by greed. It was a call to choose sides, and my allegiance was with the Common Man, so I turned my back on money.

Knowing something about their stories, I can see now why my friends, family, and neighbors had come to adopt this anti-money perspective. I can also see how my childhood mind may have warped a more innocent message into this rather cynical version of the world. I care about justice and equality, yet I witnessed money being used as an arbitrary divider and a means of exploitation. I value autonomy and creativity, but I experienced the need for money as a stifling drain on my energies (long hours at low-paying jobs do not create an ideal setting for creativity and innovation).

However it came to be formed, the power of this core belief was tremendous. My disdain for money and the financial world led me to choose the low-paying road over and over again, even as my skills and talents grew more valuable. I sabotaged my own financial progress because I believed that money had the power to corrupt me.

When I decided to go to an elite private business school to study financial planning, I was afraid to tell my family. I knew what they would think: I had gone over to the dark side. But 10 years of supporting myself without financial knowledge had taught me one important thing: If you don't pay attention to money, it will rule your life. By not learning about money, and not considering finances in my career choices, I had fewer opportunities and less autonomy in my daily life. By avoiding money, I was choosing to continue the familiar pattern of lack and financial anxiety.

I made the decision to take control of my financial life, but it was not book knowledge or estate-planning techniques that changed me— it was psychology. In my own financial narrative, I had confused injustice and inequality with money itself. In essence, I was blaming an inanimate object with no power of its own for the choices that some people were making with their stores of it. My indignation needed an outlet, but my anger was misplaced. Once I understood my mistake, I was able to separate my frustration from the concept of money and place it more productively on the systems and human frailties that create and perpetuate exploitation and corruption. Only then could I see money for what it truly is: a simple tool.

Money itself is a neutral resource, full of possibilities. It can be used for good or for ill, and how a person uses it is entirely a matter of personal choice. Once I understood what money is, and what it is not, I was able to break the habits of self-sabotage that had dogged me since childhood. I was finally free to create a life of great value without compromising my personal values.

Your experience will be unique.

In the 10 years since my journey into the world of financial psychology began, I have continued to plumb the depths of this fascinating and important topic in order to learn more about how smart, talented people can get in the way of their own financial goals. I have studied accounting, finance, economics, and consumer, social, and cognitive psychology, and I have researched how several different psychological factors contribute to (or stand in the way of) good money management. More than this, I have counseled and taught individuals, couples, small business owners, students, parents, professionals, and teachers with myriad financial challenges and needs. In every case, there is a story that runs parallel to the numbers. Those stories are as unique as the individuals who crafted them, but each plays a powerful, yet often unconscious, role in the financial decisions they make. By working with the story first, I have found that the numbers change more easily, and that change is more likely to be permanent.

This book is divided under two major themes, one abstract and one concrete. Chapters 1 through 3 give a broad overview of money and its place in our lives as a cultural and social phenomenon. These chapters are intended to give you a glimpse into the roots of your own financial narrative, and identify any problematic patterns of thinking that may be contributing to an unhealthy relationship with money. While many people want to jump immediately into making a new financial plan, I believe that first examining the beliefs you currently hold, and challenging those that may be sabotaging your success, is an important first step toward true financial freedom.

Chapter 4 offers a new framework for working with your personal finances. This budgeting structure, which I call the LOADED budget, incorporates several principles from psychology that are missing or misaligned in traditional budgeting methods. This money management method offers a way of changing your financial life by creating a plan for your money that is both deeply satisfying and also sustainable over the long term. However, since the LOADED budget incorporates psychology, it is best used after you have taken a good look at your personal beliefs and how they may manifest in your current financial choices. You may, of course, skip ahead to this section if you find the background psychology uninteresting, but I believe that you will have a more meaningful experience if you read the book cover to cover.

Along the way, you will read many people's stories. Not all are recorded as exact factual accounts; in some cases, they are meant simply to illustrate beliefs and experiences that are common to many people. In some instances, I have combined several people's stories into one narrative. In every case, the names have been changed to protect the privacy of the people involved. If there is a quotation in a personal account, however, you can trust it is a direct quote.

Last, it is important to note that personal change is not an effortless task. Because everyone has their own story, because none but you can unearth your core beliefs, because there is no shortcut past introspection, no scan to pinpoint the significant moments that shaped your thoughts about money, and no silver bullet to end financial trouble . . . because change takes effort, this book alone will not transform you. It cannot.

The pages that follow are meant to set you on a path of discovery and understanding that leads to more peace and satisfaction in your financial life. What you bring to the fore will determine your experience.

When It Comes to Money, We've All Got Issues

WE KNOW WE have problems with money. As individuals we know it, and as a country we know it. Private and public foundations spend millions of dollars every year trying to teach people how to budget, save, invest, and get out of debt. There's just one problem: It doesn't seem to be working.

Everyone has a theory as to why. One camp says it's because people are apathetic and don't care to learn. Another says it's because we aren't taught about money from an early age. I think it's because most of the financial management programs out there speak to our balance sheets, not to our *minds*.

Financial management workshops and investment classes feel irrelevant to many people. What does it matter how much you can earn at 10 percent interest over 40 years if you're struggling just to pay your grocery bill? So much of the material in financial workshops is so remote, so far from our current reality, that it's easy to check out mentally. If you can't go home and put it to use right away, what does it matter? It's just another math class.

That's why I made a promise to myself as a financial educator that as much as possible, I would not use numbers. Don't misunderstand; I love numbers. Still, learning about numbers didn't solve my financial problems. Learning about myself did that. Of course, to manage your money well you will need to do some number crunching, eventually. Regardless, I honestly believe that for most of us money management is less about numbers and more about the *stories we tell ourselves* because of those numbers. Money carries deep cultural and social meaning for each of us, and we each have developed an attitude about it based on those narratives. The decisions we make concerning money are profoundly affected by the cultural, social, and emotional meaning we attach to it, yet most financial educators completely ignore these aspects. Instead, we are taught about money as if all of our financial decisions were made in the sterile environment of a classroom, with our calculators at the ready and our rational minds playing absolute commander over our passions and desires. This is not the case at all. The entire field of behavioral economics is based on the growing body of evidence that people are not always rational when making financial decisions. Despite the waves this notion made in the field of economics, it comes as a surprise to pretty much no one.

> *Money is probably the most emotionally meaningful object in contemporary life; only food and sex are its close competitors as common carriers of such strong and diverse feelings, significances, and strivings.*
>
> —David W. Krueger, MD[1]

The reality is that we make our financial decisions in the context of our wider lives. Every purchase, payment, investment, or gift takes place within the larger picture that encompasses our work, our families, our obligations, our ambitions, and our feelings, hopes, struggles, and frustrations.

To navigate through the enormous complexity of our lives, we take shortcuts and develop rules of thumb and simple narratives to guide us. This is an adaptive trait that helps us to make quick decisions and easily understand the world around us. The problem comes when the narratives intended to guide us actually work against us, or stand in the way of reaching our goals. When this happens, we need tools to help us rewrite those stories and get back on the path to our best future.

With this in mind, we will begin by taking a look at the environment where all of our financial lives began. A person's core beliefs and financial stories have their roots in the individual relationships, the environment, and the events they have experienced. It is certainly true that we have all had unique circumstances, role models, and experiences with money, so no book can speak directly to your background. Yet, one thing is fairly universal: Money is a loaded topic in our culture. So loaded, in fact, that it is the world's most impolite subject.

Note

1. David W. Krueger, "Money, Success, and Success Phobia," in *The Last Taboo: Money as a Symbol & Reality in Psychotherapy & Psychoanalysis,* ed. David W. Krueger (New York: Brunner/Mazel, 1986), 3.

2

Money Messages

> *Money never stays with me. It would burn me if it did. I throw it out of my hands as soon as possible, lest it find its way into my heart.*
>
> —John Wesley, cofounder of the Methodist Church

We Don't Talk about Money

Do you want shut down conversations, lose friends, and alienate people? It's very simple, really. Just ask someone how much money they make.

More than religion or politics, more than personal health problems, more than taxes, and even more than death, people rank money as the single most uncomfortable topic of conversation. According to a survey published by Wells Fargo in 2014, nearly half of the people polled said that money was the most difficult topic to talk about. It's not surprising, really. In the modern Western world, a society that highly values independence and personal success, we know that as soon as a number is spoken, judgments will follow. What's more, we seem to understand intuitively that a person's views about money are deeply linked to their overall value system, and differences in opinion about how much is enough, or too much, can quickly create a cavernous divide between friends.[1]

Contrary to popular belief, the rich don't talk about money any more than the poor. Quite often when I speak to groups about financial psychology and money management, people bemoan the injustice that children who grow up in wealthy households are far more equipped to handle money when they are grown than their lower-income peers. There is a popular misconception that wealthy parents do a better job of teaching their children about money management than the poor. Beloved books such as *Rich Dad, Poor Dad* capitalize on this fallacy, but it is simply not true. In June 2015, the *New York Times* published an article[2] by Ron Lieber reporting the results of a survey of wealthy parents that debunks this popular myth. In fact, only 17 percent of the parents surveyed said that they have told or would tell their children about their income or net worth by the time they reached 18 years of age. When asked why, nearly a third simply said it was "none of their business." That doesn't sound like open financial communication to me.

If the wealthy were really better at discussing money with their children, then we might not see as many instances of the famed "shirtsleeves to shirtsleeves in three generations" phenomenon. As far back as anyone can tell, there has been a cycle of wealth: One generation earns it, the next generation spends it, and the third generation is left to start over. Nearly every culture in the world has a term for it, showing that this is not a new or American experience. In Italian, they say, "From stalls to stars to stalls." In Japan, it's, "The third generation ruins the house." In China, they simply say, "Wealth does not survive three generations." The pattern of wealth created and wealth lost in three generations has persisted across cultures and time. Yes, there are some families who have managed to carry wealth through many generations, but there is far less "old money" in this world than many think. If wealthy parents were truly better at teaching money management to their children, I doubt very much that this pattern would have persisted. The truth is most people simply don't talk about money.

If nobody is talking about money, then how do we learn about it? The evidence suggests that on the whole we really don't learn very much. Annamaria Lusardi, arguably one of the most prominent experts on financial literacy in America, created a simple test of basic financial concepts called the Big Five Financial Literacy Questions. These five questions cover several very simple financial concepts like interest, inflation, and risk. As simple as this little quiz may be, when the Treasury presented it to a cross section of Americans, only 15 percent answered them all correctly. Think you can do better? You can take a look at the Big Five as well as a simple explanation of each question in the self-assessment section at the end of this book (Appendix A). Even a three-question version, which covered only the most basic concepts, had a dismal pass rate.

Our general lack of financial knowledge may be due to our reluctance to openly discuss financial matters, or it might be the other way around; maybe we hesitate to talk about money because we don't want to reveal our lack of knowledge. Either way, the problem remains. In polite society, we simply do not discuss money.

Or do we?

We Talk about Money Constantly

Discussing money and class may be taboo, but we actually do it all the time. We don't do it with words, exactly, but through thousands of little unspoken social cues. Where we live, what we wear, what schools we attend or send our children to, what we drive, where we shop, what words we use, what causes we support, and to what extent we give all send messages to others about where we fall on the socioeconomic ladder.

Children pick up on these money messages quickly, and incorporate them into their own personal narratives. One man I spoke to told me about his experiences with class growing up in an upper-middle-class town in Maryland:

I vividly recall my experience riding the school bus in grade school where early on I was exposed to the stress and anxiety of wanting to fit in and being accepted by my peers. I was raised in a small trailer, and on my street there were lots of rich kids with big homes. I would see the pools, designer clothes, and dirt bikes, and at that early age I decided that I would be wealthy one day. My family was not poor by any means as my parents worked long hours at a family-run printing business to make a respectable income, and we always had more than we needed. On Christmas, our living room would be overflowing with gifts, so that what we lacked in a home was made up in other ways.

As a young child I remember being fearful that the kids would find out that I lived in a trailer, and that word would get back to my classmates. Our trailer was fifty feet from my grandparents' house. It was an older, modest farmhouse. So, if anyone on the bus asked, I would pretend like that was where we lived. It was a daily stress riding the bus that my secret would one day be revealed.

This little boy lived with daily stress based on unspoken money messages that told him he would be rejected if people knew he lived in a trailer. What strikes me the most about this story is the fact that, given his fear of his classmates learning where he lived, he probably didn't invite his friends from school over to play. Money messages were already shaping his behavior, and the financial narrative he believed was causing him to lie and put limits on his social life.

Money messages permeate every part of society. They are in our songs, films, and literature. They are planted deep within our psyches as children in the form of fairy tales and rags-to-riches stories. They are made real when, at school age, we are judged by the brands we wear and the homes we live in. They are further strengthened as adults when we date, socialize, or attend church. Money messages are everywhere. Some are subtle, some are not; some are positive, some are not; but they all play their part in shaping our experiences and attitudes toward money.

The first step to having a healthy relationship with money is to get some clarity about the money messages to which you personally have been exposed, and to figure out which ones you took to heart, and how they are serving you today.

From Freud to Frodo: The Stories We Tell Each Other

Sigmund Freud believed that the human psyche draws a parallel between money and feces. He was Freud, after all; some things are to be expected. While Freud's interpretation may strike some as odd, the idea that we have some cultural or subconscious metaphors for money is not the least bit strange. Ask an economist, and they will tell you that money is a "store of value," or a "medium of exchange," but economists are probably the only ones who will take such a sterile tone. Far from these emotionless descriptions, most cultural interpretations of money tend to describe it as falling into either the category of the sacred or the profane. Nearly every money message we encounter has within it some tone of good or evil, and taking stock of which messages we have come to believe, and the moral tenor they imply, can bring us a long way toward understanding why we behave the way we do with our own money. Realizing the moral undertone of the messages we have internalized can also help explain why so many of us have a love–hate relationship with money, or have come to consider it a "necessary evil."

Money messages surround us in our cultural stories, proverbs, fables, and pithy words of wisdom. These stories tend to fall into three broad categories. First, there are the words of wisdom that we hear again and again in the form of proverbs or common sayings. I think of these stories as messages about money disguised as advice about life.

Money doesn't grow on trees.
Money makes the world go 'round.
Money is the root of all evil.
Money can't buy me love.
A penny saved is a penny earned.
Mo' money, mo' problems.

This is the most obvious kind of money message, and the easiest to spot. You may be able to add to the list with a few that your parents, grandparents, or teachers said to you. They may seem silly or inconsequential, but these pithy little nuggets often have a powerful effect in shaping our core beliefs.

For example, "Money doesn't grow on trees" is meant, at its best, to encourage people to value money and not waste it. On the other hand, this saying also sends a strong message of scarcity. Rather than just an admonition to appreciate the value of money, this message can be taken to mean that money is rare or difficult to come by. If you believe as a child that it is hard to make money, how will you approach work? Will you feel sure of your ability to support yourself? Will you see money as something you can have personally, or will you view it as something you will struggle to obtain?

"Money is the root of all evil" is another classic money message. It is actually a very famous misquote of the Bible. The real beginning of the verse, according to the King James Version, is, *"For the love of money is the root of all evil."* (1 Timothy 6:10.) This sends a very different message. The first blames money itself for the evils in the world. The second blames people with greed in their hearts. Subtle differences like this can make an enormous difference in how we view the world, and this particular message—that money itself is responsible for the darkness in our world—is one that many people seem to have taken to heart. John Wesley, who I quoted at the outset of this section, certainly did.

These messages are fairly simple to separate into the categories of "Money is good," and "Money is bad," because they are clear, verbal representations of moral judgments on money. Some may have mixed ethical implications such as "Money is power," which could be good or bad, depending on your feelings about power. Still, most often when I hear people say this, it is a part of a larger statement that goes something like, "Money is power, and power corrupts. Therefore, money corrupts." According to this view, money is like the Ring of Mordor in J.R.R. Tolkien's famous novels, threatening to destroy the hearts of any who hold on to it too long because of the power that it affords its owner. Again, the moral lesson in the money message is clear.

Other money messages are less obvious because they are not spoken verbally, but woven into stories. These can take the form of stories with caricatures depicting the wealthy as sickening, black-hearted pigs with no humanity, while the poor are drawn as glorious models of virtue. We see the same characters again and again in stories spanning from ancient to modern times. King Midas, Ebenezer Scrooge, Mr. Burns, and Mr. Krabs are the same recycled character. They represent the person who cares for money above all. Whether soulless or simply misguided, they represent a person we should not aspire to be. This character type is an example of misplaced priorities.

On the other hand, stories of those who maintain pure hearts in impoverished situations and receive a helping hand from the gods or Fate are also quite popular. Oliver Twist, Aladdin, The Tramp from the Disney movie, Cinderella, and Charlie Bucket (of *Charlie and the Chocolate Factory*) are all embodiments of the humble heart that Fate steps in to save. Ironically, how does Fate save them? By making them wealthy. We do love our rags-to-riches stories.

While these stories and characters have some very positive lessons to teach, they can also have a poisonous effect if we are not careful to guard ourselves against the influence of the stereotypes that they paint. We should all take to heart the warnings against becoming dispassionate toward our fellows, and keep our hearts unsullied by greed, but these stories are often incredibly simplistic in their depictions of the heroes and villains. It is easy to paint all wealthy men as Ebenezer Scrooges and all poor boys as Charlie Buckets; however, in doing so we not only reduce human beings to caricatures, but we also risk sabotaging our own financial well-being. When we equate wealth with greed, and poverty with goodness, we can unwittingly start to believe that the only way to be a good person and still have wealth is to be granted a gift of Fate like these characters were.

The theme of good people shunning money, yet being granted wealth and ease by the hand of Fate, is pervasive in our cultural stories. Yes, it is true that these stories often shed light on the injustice of the economic status quo, but they also send a message that is, in my opinion, a very dangerous one. They subtly suggest that a person can either care about people *or* they can care about money. They have a subtle but profound undertone of financial moralism that judges money as indecent and calls us to choose sides. "Good things happen to good people," they seem to claim, but money is only considered a "good thing" if it is unintentionally gotten as a reward for a good heart.

The third type of story we tell each other about who we are is through the subtle and not-so-subtle social cues I mentioned previously—in this case little unspoken economic cues. For example, I recently met a woman who told me about the complex emotional experience she had when she lost her engagement ring.

Kathy's Story

When Kathy lost her diamond ring, she was understandably distraught. Over the course of two days, she went through the normal stages of grief. Denial: She would find it, for sure. Anger: How could she be so stupid to lose such an important thing? Depression: The most important symbol of her early days with her spouse was gone for good. . . . And, then there was Bargaining: Should she buy a replacement?

Here, the social part of this symbol of love shone through. One of the hardest parts of losing her diamond engagement band was not the loss of a treasured gift. As her husband sweetly, if tactlessly, reminded her, "You never liked it that much, anyway." When she lost her ring, Kathy came face to face with the fact that having those diamonds on her finger was a kind of social currency. She and her family lived in a very affluent neighborhood, and the private school that her children attended attracted some of the wealthiest families in the country. Her ring was more than a symbol of love from her husband. It was also a sign of belonging in that world. Without it, she worried that the other mothers she knew from the neighborhood and school would see her in a less favorable light. I half-jokingly suggested that perhaps these women would appreciate understatement as a show of class. She said, "One friend of mine, God love her, said once, 'If it's less than two carats, don't bother. I won't wear it." Understatement was, apparently, not their thing.

Kathy found her ring on the third day, and so she was spared the dilemma of whether or not to replace it. Before you write Kathy's experience off as a petty problem, remember the little boy who lived in the trailer and was afraid to tell his friends. The same dynamic is at play in both situations. We all need to belong. If we don't have the same things as those around us, we know we risk being seen as somehow not measuring up. It is an evolutionary trait that we feel secure with people who are like us; you're less likely to be attacked by your own group. It is a very scary thing to find yourself without the markings of your tribe.

This dynamic can work in the opposite direction, too. Kids who leave their low-income neighborhoods behind to pursue higher education or better job prospects often pay a high social cost. Many bright young scholars who leave the projects to attend prestigious colleges find themselves feeling isolated and alone. Coming from a different background, they often don't fit in at their new school, and when they go home they can find themselves ostracized for "forgetting their roots." I vividly remember one high school senior who attended a seminar I taught in rural Maine. He was living on his own at 17, something I myself did in my senior year. He rejected the idea that college was a real option for him and his classmates on the grounds that their parents didn't want it to happen. "Rednecks don't want college kids," he said.

This shocked me at first until I understood that these kids' parents didn't want to see their children move away. They preferred that they struggle nearby and maintain their close relationships over letting them go where they could find more work, but be in less frequent contact. The threat of being rejected for trying to get ahead financially can lead some people to decide that it is better to live in poverty among friends than to be financially successful, but alone.

Money messages are everywhere. They are in our homes, on our televisions and movie screens; they shout at us from billboards, and whisper to us through social norms. We are steeped in money messages before we can speak, and by the time we are adults, often without our knowing, they have matured into personal narratives and core beliefs. The stories that we tell each other eventually become the stories that we tell ourselves.

The Stories We Tell Ourselves

As we grow and mature, the money messages we are exposed to combine with our experiences to create a personal, evidence-based narrative about money. For some of us, there are critical, defining moments that instill within us certain financial beliefs. For others, our narratives grow slowly and imperceptibly as we age. We all have a narrative, but often we don't realize what it is until we are asked to articulate it.

The money messages we absorb, the role models we observe, and the circumstances in which we were born and raised all combine to shape the stories we eventually tell ourselves about money, its role in the world and in our own lives, and whether it is a friend or an enemy, good or evil. I interviewed several people from diverse backgrounds and asked them about their financial stories. As you read these anecdotes, ask yourself, would you have come to the same conclusions? If these circumstances were your own, would your narrative be different?

"Money Is a Betrayer": Adina's Story

Adina grew up in the 1950s in what she describes as a middle-class, white neighborhood. Her father thought that working for anyone else was "white slavery," so he made continuous attempts at self-employment, though as Adina recalls, "he was no good at it." As a result, Adina's family was dependent on her mother, who worked as a teacher during the school year and as a secretary during the summers. Her mother resented the obligation, and it created a constant undercurrent of stress in the household. In addition to this, Adina's brother had polio, and his surgeries and physical therapy were a financial strain on the family. At a young age, Adina felt guilty for being an additional burden on her already overworked mother. "I tried to make up for the problems by not needing anything, and by earning whatever I could, almost obsessively," she recalls. She began working at 14, and once she graduated, she consistently worked two jobs until she married.

Throughout her adult life, Adina has worked and saved, but she has also faced bitter legal battles with a now ex-husband who, she says, has sued her dozens of times on various grounds. The legal fees alone have swallowed her life's savings and the $100,000 that her mother left when she passed. In Adina's experience, it seems that every time she has managed to create a sense of financial security for herself, she has been hit with another lawsuit, and watched that security disappear again. At 68, she now lives on Social Security, with "not even enough extra to see a movie once a week."

As a child, she thought that earning money would bring her security. She now feels betrayed by money because she found that having it, rather than providing security, made her a target for the greed of others.

"The Money in My Life Is Cursed": Eric's Story

Eric's early life was pleasant, but modest. He was part of a large family; there was always enough, but never any extra. He looked forward to the days when he would be free to earn his own living and get ahead financially. As a young professional, he was happy to be taking that step into financial security—something his parents had worked hard to help him achieve.

Over time, though, Eric started to notice a strange pattern. As soon as he built up his savings, some unexpected, large expense would surface. In 2008, his stock options at his company matured, giving him just enough to make the down payment on a house. The very day that he intended to make an offer on a home that he loved, he got the news that he was to be laid off due to downsizing. Another time, he received an unexpected tax refund of $3,000 only to learn days later that his car needed more than $2,000 in repairs.

The pattern was so real to Eric that he began to dread having extra money. "Now, when I unexpectedly find myself feeling comfortable, all I can think is, 'Oh, no. What huge expense is on its way to take this money away?'" Not only does Eric see this pattern recurring in his life, he has found a way to explain it. "Growing up, we had just enough, and it seems I always have just enough now. Whenever I have more than enough, it gets taken away by chance, so maybe I'm *supposed* to have just enough and no more." Our minds want to make sense of the patterns we see. We crave meaning, even if we don't like the story the patterns tell us.

"Money Is Power, and Power Corrupts": Matthew's Story

After growing up feeling like he lived in the shadow of the wealthy, Matthew was determined to be rich. He discovered in high school that his intellectual aptitude was his ticket to wealth, and so he worked hard and became the first person in his family to earn a college degree. Graduating in the wake of 9/11, he found work as an IT engineer for the Department of Defense, and spent 10 years climbing up the socio-economic ladder. As he tells it:

> I was able to save and invest aggressively and in time I developed a new sense of peace in terms of my financial status. I was able to do things I enjoyed like travel with my family and dine out at high-end restaurants. I traded stocks frequently and made a lot of money as the technology sector grew by leaps and bounds. I was a proficient saver with the goal of living off of passive income and my wealth grew rapidly within a few years. I also invested heavily in real estate. I eventually owned and operated four rental properties in the DC region.

Then, the real estate market crashed. Matthew saw his fortunes crumble, and developed depression and a substance abuse problem. He eventually filed for bankruptcy, and began to start over. Within a few years, he had saved over $100,000 and had paid off all his remaining debts. Then, while back on top, something inside him broke:

> I ended up repeating the same cycle of depression, illness, and substance abuse, quitting my job, and then ended up on the fringe of being on the streets with my family. Shortly after quitting my job I burned through my savings again and got arrested twice for DUI. I lost my government clearance, career, health, home, car, family relationships, self-esteem, and ultimately my identity and purpose. I ended up in a homeless shelter.

We read about Matthew earlier—he was the little boy on the bus who feared being found out for living in a trailer. Matthew attributes much of his experience to the feelings of power that came along with money and accomplishment. As the first college graduate in his family, he was granted respect and influence. As a financially successful person, he felt the increase of influence that others allowed him to have over them, and he says his ego grew along with their esteem. He wasn't emotionally prepared to handle the experience of having power over others while staying grounded in his own values. Now, while he is working hard to get back to mental, emotional, and financial stability, he is taking the lessons he learned at "rock bottom" with him. He believes that by volunteering, and staying connected to the less fortunate, he may be able to avoid the emotional traps that previously got the best of him.

"Stability Will Not Remain Forever": Nicholas's Story

Nicholas has had a self-described love–hate relationship with money all his life. As a child, he reacted to the financial stress he saw around him by promising himself to be a high earner when he grew up, and he succeeded. The experiences of his childhood stuck with him, however. Even when his income began to allow him a level of financial comfort he had only dreamed of as a child, he still felt a constant undercurrent of insecurity. What if it all went away? He described his financial experience as "comfortable, with plenty of disposable income" and yet tarnished by a "constant, nagging doubt." The fear of experiencing financial stress is so deep inside him that no matter how much he earns, he never feels safe. On top of these fears, once he had significant assets to manage, he realized that he didn't know how, which added to his sense of insecurity. What if his own lack of knowledge led him back into financial stress? His childhood dream of comfort has been harder to reach than he imagined because he didn't account for the deep, unconscious fears that would eventually haunt him even as he accomplished his financial goals. Peace of mind involves more than just the numbers on our balance sheet.

"Money Ruins Relationships": Jillian's Story

I cannot do Jillian's background justice, so I will let her tell it:

> I have had a very difficult relationship with money since I was a child. I grew up with a single mom who did everything she could to bring food to the table; however, her job didn't pay too much, so a lot of times we skipped meals, and I even remember myself looking for pennies in the house we lived in to go and buy at least one egg for me and my little brother. My mother made great sacrifices trying to give us everything we needed. She worked in a fast-food restaurant and she wouldn't eat her food only to take it to me so I can have something

to eat. It was a really hard time. When I was a big girl, I remember wanting to have pretty things other girls had, like some nice shoes and stuff. We lacked so much money that my mom could not buy feminine pads, so we both had to use pieces of fabric to act like one. It was really hard!

Jillian put herself through college and worked hard to create some financial stability for herself, including buying her own home as a single woman. When she married, her husband insisted that she stop working. He would pay the bills and provide for her. She thought that life would be easier than it had been before.

Unfortunately, Jillian's husband has very different financial priorities than she does, and this union has not brought her the relief she thought it would. Jillian now has access to money only at her husband's discretion. He provides her with a very small "allowance" and insists that she not work, even though she very much wants to. She wants to create a college fund for their children and get a decent haircut for herself. Even though she is "taken care of" by her husband, Jillian feels deprived almost constantly because according to the rules of her home, she is not allowed things that she knows she could easily afford. "He doesn't allow me to buy things for myself, only for the family," she says. Her husband's attitudes toward money and family roles have all but ended their relationship. "I cannot help the grudge I hold toward him for being so cheap with me," Jillian says. She sees her husband as someone who cares far more about money than the people in his life, and it has destroyed her warm feelings for him.

Stories Can Help or Hurt

As much as we do not discuss money in detail in our culture, I have found that given a safe space and a nonjudgmental listener, people are very willing to open up. One of the benefits of my work is hearing so many colorful, painful, surprising, and sometimes beautiful stories about people's financial lives. I have heard about terrible injustices committed for money: bullying, theft, and the like. I have heard people talk about their most inspiring role models and seen their eyes light up as they describe the person who made such a strong impact on them. There are a couple of trends that I have noticed over the years, one of which I believe is important to mention in the context of our personal narratives, and that is this: Many people stay in terrible, and sometimes dangerous, situations because they do not have the confidence that they could survive financially on their own.

Staying in a loveless or destructive relationship because of financial dependence is not an experience limited to women, but it is more common among women due to traditional gender roles. There is a group called Women in Financial Education (WIFE) that has a funny/sad slogan: "A man is not a financial plan." I love this slogan, but it highlights a real problem. Not just women, but anyone who is dependent on another person financially, may be tempted to compromise their true values out of fear of not being able to make it on their own. In my own experience, when my marriage began to unravel, it was only when I knew that I had enough money saved to survive the transition to single motherhood that I was emotionally able to take the plunge. I have a lot of empathy for the people who feel trapped in unhappy situations for financial reasons, and I encourage everyone, regardless of the role they wish to play in a family (breadwinner, homemaker, etc.), to have some personal savings, or at the very least to have a skill they can use to get a good job if it becomes necessary. There is incredible personal freedom in knowing that you *can* support yourself, even if you choose to rely on another. This includes the freedom to stay with your partner, but out of devotion, not desperation.

There is also an interesting and somewhat dark irony that has emerged as I interview more and more people about their financial narratives. It is clear from the preceding stories that each person has a very emotionally charged relationship with money. Yet when I asked these same people how they would explain money to a child, they immediately removed all emotion and started using phrases like, "Money is useful for meeting your needs" and "Money is a means of trade." In reality, we experience money in complex and highly emotional ways, yet when it comes to teaching the next generation about money, suddenly we all start talking like economists! One man explained that he would not want a child to know the social implications of money, only its purpose as a unit of currency. I understand the desire to protect the innocent from unpleasant truths, but the difference between the book definition of money and its actual impact on our lives is enormous. Are we really teaching our children about money if we leave out any discussion of class?

Surely, the generation that raised us was not much different. They also had complex, emotional financial lives, and we watched them play out. Yet if they talked to us about money at all, they probably just told us, "Money is a means of exchange." No wonder we are all so confused and unprepared.

Heuristics and Biases Shape Our Stories

Even though our personal narratives are often based on many years of experience and may involve a large cast of characters, they can usually be distilled to one simple sentence that reflects a core belief about money. Our tendency to reduce larger experiences to core beliefs and takeaways is part of what makes us capable of doing so much with our lives. It's a way of making sense of an incredibly complex world. When events happen to us, we take them into our store of experience and look for patterns in order to develop rules of thumb. This makes navigating the world a little easier.

Behavioral economists call these rules of thumb *heuristics*, and they can be wonderful things. They make our lives simpler by reducing the cognitive load that we have to bear when we make a decision or enter into new, uncharted situations. One of these shortcuts is known as the *availability heuristic*, and it is meant to help us make predictions about which outcomes are likely to happen and which are not.

For example, what is the likelihood that the next car you see will be red?

To answer this, your mind may go to the last time you saw cars. How many were red? Your mind's tactic for answering this question is to draw on recent experiences. What are the most readily available examples that come to mind? This gives you a sense of the probability of the next car you see being red.

This mental shortcut can come in handy, but it can also lead us to false conclusions. Rare and surprising things often stick in our memory longer than the mundane, leading us to overestimate their likelihood. In a world where the unlikeliest events are broadcast the most often, and in the most places, we end up exposed to the existence of rare events more frequently than we would encounter them in the normal course of living our lives. Highly emotional or shocking events will be remembered with much more intensity than common ones, and therefore be called to mind easier. On the other hand, we can sometimes fail even to notice frequent, commonplace events, leading us to underestimate their likelihood. This shortcut of thinking that the things we can call to mind more easily are therefore more likely can actually skew our predictions of what is likely and what is not. It can lead people to spend thousands of dollars a year on lottery tickets, for example, when that money would serve them far better by being invested in mutual funds.

Another shortcut we use a lot is called *confirmation bias*. Confirmation bias is our tendency to pay more attention to information that supports what we already believe. We don't like to go through the hassle of rewriting our personal narratives. It can be aggravating and takes mental and emotional effort. We strongly prefer to be reassured that the conclusions we have already drawn are correct, and go on our merry way. This can disrupt our financial lives by making us feel very sure that our views of money are not just opinions based on our limited experiences, but deeply and profoundly true. Once we form a personal narrative based on the money messages we believe, we will pay more attention to the information and events we encounter that support that narrative, and ignore or discredit examples that challenge them.

Mental shortcuts like the availability heuristic and confirmation bias take hold of our personal narratives, and help to turn them into core beliefs. The decisions we make are heavily influenced by what we believe, so if we want to make changes in our financial behavior, we have to examine our core beliefs.

Identifying Core Beliefs
You might think that if something is a core belief then it must already be obvious to us, but this isn't always the case. Sometimes our beliefs are deep within our unconscious understanding of life. If your beliefs about money

are not immediately obvious to you, how do you go about uncovering them? Writing your financial story can help. I find that writing is better than just thinking about it because by writing things down, we tend to create some sort of storyline, whereas when we just think of our financial story, we can see a jumble of mental images and events without much of a meaningful arc. Our core beliefs are more apparent when we look at the stories we are telling ourselves, so I encourage you to write your story down.

To help you do so, think about this: Up to this point, if money were a character in your life's story, would it be a friend or an enemy? You can also think about the money messages you were told or otherwise exposed to growing up. What were your parents' attitudes about money? Who were your greatest financial influences, for good or bad? Like the little boy on the school bus who decided he would be rich one day because he hated the feeling of having less than the people around him and feared their judgment, were there any defining moments that triggered strong emotional responses within you? Did the people who surrounded you growing up view money as good or evil? How do you feel now when you think about the money in your life? Have you made any financial promises to yourself? All of these questions can help you write out your story. There is also a worksheet at the end of the book to help you through this process.

The financial stories I've shared from other people are quite short, but the interviews they are taken from were far more lengthy and detailed. I encourage you to really take the time to think through your financial experiences from early childhood until now. Look for the patterns you have come to find meaningful. There is a narrative inside of you, and a story you are telling yourself. That story already influences your financial decisions because it is based on your core beliefs. By finding and articulating the story, you are one step closer to uncovering your core beliefs about money. Then, and only then, can you decide if those beliefs are serving you well, or if you need to challenge them.

Challenging Core Beliefs

Once you know your story, it will give you clues about your core beliefs. Was money a friend or an enemy in your story? Was it a hero or a villain? In your story, where is the power? Does a higher power rule the day, or are you in the driver's seat? If your story were a fable, what would the "moral" be at the end? Try to put the lesson of your financial story into one sentence. This is a core financial belief.

The greatest turning point in my financial life came when I discovered my core beliefs about money. By writing about my experiences with money from early childhood up to that point (in my late twenties), I found that the two most influential money messages that I was holding on to at the time had sort of merged themselves into one core belief: "I am not *supposed* to have money because it is evil."

It was a powerful awakening to see these words written out so simply. Did I really believe this? Yes, I realized, I did believe it. I believed it so deeply, in fact, that not only had I avoided focusing on making money, but whenever I had extra money I spent it or gave it away. I had thought this was because I was either irresponsible or generous (or both), but in fact it's because I was scared. I felt exactly as John Wesley did when he said, "Money never stays with me. It would burn me if it did. I throw it out of my hands as soon as possible, lest it find its way into my heart." In fact, whenever I had anything more than I personally needed for survival, I felt deeply guilty. Even a very small amount of savings made me feel as if I were personally taking food out of the mouths of people who needed that money more than I did. My early religious upbringing, my experiences with lack as a child, and all of the examples of injustice and inequality I had witnessed in the world around me had combined in my mind to create a narrative where money was a perpetrator of evil, and I wanted nothing to do with that.

Once I saw how much of an enemy I had made money into in my mental narrative, I finally understood how that one belief had led me to countless acts of financial self-sabotage. For example, at 22, I had been offered a recording contract. Up to that point, this had been my life's greatest dream. Instead of jumping for joy and accepting the opportunity, I froze. The producer was talking about some big numbers. He wanted me to get comfortable with the idea of riding in a limousine. His talk reminded me of the stereotypical rich characters I had come to loathe, and I was terrified that I would be selling out if

I followed that path. The "starving artist" stories came to mind as examples of people who were pure-hearted and true to their art, and he sounded like the fat cat who ate starving artists for breakfast. I turned it down. I could have had my dream career at 22. I could have made a living doing what I loved at a very early age, and I turned it down because of the stories I was telling myself about money.

What happens when our stories lead us to self-sabotage? We need to change them. The most important thing to remember about our financial stories is this: They are just stories. In the words of Louise Hay, "It's only a thought, and a thought can change." Which of your core financial beliefs might be holding you back from living your best life? If you have found a belief that you think might be hurting you, how do you go about changing it? I have found two strategies that can help.

Strategy 1: Change the Narrative

If possible, can you change your financial narrative so that the moral of the story is different? Think about Eric, who saw that every time he saved up a chunk of money, some large expense drained his account. He concluded that his money was cursed, and began to feel a sense of dread when unexpected money came his way. He believed that some larger force did not want him to have anything more than he needed. A different interpretation might have been to feel incredibly lucky that somehow he always had money to pay for life's surprise expenses. Even when he hadn't planned or saved up in advance, he seemed to always get a sudden windfall that helped cover him in emergencies. This belief might lead Eric to feel that he was blessed, not cursed. He might also decide to save more, knowing that life is always full of expensive surprises, and that it feels good to have the money on hand to cover them. In that case, rather than concluding that somehow life doesn't want him to have more than "just enough," which has an undertone of lack, his core belief might evolve to something like, "I always have enough," which has an undertone of abundance. It's a shift in interpretation of the same events, but it leads to a very different emotional experience with money, and life.

Is there a different, but still truthful, interpretation of your narrative that you could write?

Strategy 2: Find the Counterexample

Another way to challenge a core belief that is not working well for you is to use a strategy popular among mathematicians. There is a scientific process for proving mathematical statements using pure logic, and it comes in very handy when we need to challenge a deep belief. When you want to prove that a mathematical statement is true or false, you either have to show that it is true in *every case*, or you can prove it false by finding *just one case* where it is not true. When it comes to beliefs, finding *just one* case where the belief doesn't hold up can often be enough to break its hold on you. Once you find the counterexample, whenever you find yourself faced with that problematic belief, you can bring that example to mind. The counterexample will remind you that it is not *always* true, and so it may not be true in your case, either. Our minds really do respond well to logic at times.

Consider Jillian, who has come to believe that money ruins relationships because of the different financial priorities that she and her husband have. Certainly, money is a cause of strife in many relationships, and she has seen plenty of examples to support that. Still, there must be some relationships she has had that were not ruined by money. As a mother, having money allows her to care for her children. Those relationships are better off because of her resourceful use of money. Or, she could look to her particular relationship and perhaps conclude that it is not money that is ruining that bond, but a conflict over priorities.

In my own case, when I feared that signing a record contract would mean I had "sold out" as an artist, thinking of just one example of a popular artist who has personally stirred my own soul through their music might have helped me combat my fears. If that artist could make money and still keep their music soulful, then maybe I could as well. Think about your core beliefs, and then ask yourself, "Is there a single example where this is *not* true?"

Using Science to Our Advantage

Changing core beliefs is not easy, but it is possible. In addition to the beliefs and attitudes that we carry regarding money, there are a number of other mental factors that research shows can either help or hurt us when we make financial decisions. As someone with a personal history of making money mistakes by letting unexamined beliefs interfere with my financial life, I became extremely interested in what other ways people might unwittingly sabotage their financial well-being. This question became the driving motivation behind my doctoral research. I wanted to know how and why otherwise smart people can get in their own way financially. While I certainly do not know everything there is to know about this topic, I have managed to uncover some very interesting and useful themes. The next section will give a very brief overview of some of the research on money and the mind that may help you to challenge the core beliefs that are not working for you, and reduce the impact of other mental factors that might be working against you.

Notes

1. Wells Fargo, "Conversations about Personal Finance More Difficult Than Religion and Politics, According to New Wells Fargo Survey," news release, February 20, 2014, www.wellsfargo.com/about/press/2014/20140220_financial-health/.
2. Ron Lieber, "Why Affluent Parents Clam Up about Their Incomes," *Motherlode* (blog), *New York Times*, June 24, 2015, http://parenting.blogs.nytimes.com/2015/06/24/why-affluent-parents-clam-up-about-their-incomes/?_r=2.

3

Poverty, Privilege, and Prejudice

*A Crash Course in the Science of Money
Psychology*

THIS CHAPTER LOOKS at research findings on how money affects the mind, and how our mental shortcuts can affect the way we deal with our money, and each other. Are the cultural stereotypes and money messages that surround us true? Does money corrupt? Is less really more? How does thinking about money affect a person's desire to help others? How does the way a person thinks about time relate to their financial behaviors? These and many other questions are addressed in this section.

In the next few pages, I will walk you through research that looks at how having money, or not having it, can affect your health, your relationships, and your perspective. Some of this might seem heady and complex, and you may wonder what these studies have to do with your day-to-day life and money management. The fact is that both lack and privilege can affect many parts of our psychology, and if we want to change our behaviors, we need to understand where they come from. We've talked about how our experiences with lack or wealth can shape our personal narratives. Now, we'll look at how having (or not having) money affects other parts of our minds, shaping our behavior in ways we may never have thought about before.

Since the concept of money affecting our psychology is a very sensitive topic, I have done my best to document the studies that support the claims made in this section. I want you to be able to trust the information here, and to look deeper into any finding that I mention. At the same time, I recognize that some readers may find the academic language a bit off-putting, and so I have broken the section into bite-sized pieces, and sprinkled in some real-world examples and ideas for how to apply these findings along the way. At the end of this section, you will find a list of the self-assessments, activities, and interventions that are mentioned in the text. You can use these on your own to overcome some of the challenges I outline here.

We'll look at the science of money psychology from two directions. First, I'll talk about money from the point of view of *social* psychology. You'll learn about how your socioeconomic upbringing might affect your body, mind, and the way you view yourself in relation to others. After that, I'll talk about money from the perspective of *cognitive* psychology. In this part, you'll learn how several other mental factors (like how you think about time) can affect how you manage, or mismanage, your money.

We don't all experience every aspect of money psychology. The purpose of this section is to give you concrete, scientific evidence that certain ways of thinking are helpful to our money management, while others are not, and to address the very real (but very taboo) impact of economic prejudice and its effects on our individual lives and the fabric of our social systems. The money management system presented later in the book is designed to overcome some of the challenges that I lay out in this section. To get the most out of the LOADED budget, it's helpful to understand the factors that can work against us when we are trying to manage our money well.

With that in mind, let's begin by looking at how poverty and privilege can each affect a person's psychological well-being and contribute to the formation of core beliefs.

Money and Social Psychology: How Poverty, Privilege, and Comparisons Affect Our Minds and Behavior

Research studies over the past few decades reveal an interesting paradox: Lack of money is linked to depression, relationship problems, lower performance on difficult tasks, and even shorter life expectancy, yet just thinking about money can lead to antisocial behavior and reduce compassion. It would appear that money creates a lose-lose scenario: If you don't have it, your performance suffers, your relationships suffer, and you may die sooner. But, if you have great wealth, you may be more likely to engage in victim blaming, and less likely to help others by choice.

How do we solve this conflict? Do we have to choose between caring about people and caring about money? How do we create lives of great value, without compromising our own deep values? We do it by working with our psychology. By mindfully developing a healthy relationship with money and learning some simple new ways of thinking, we can avoid the psychological dangers that can accompany both poverty and wealth.

Poverty: Why Not Having Enough Is a Major Drag

If you have grown up with core beliefs that cast money in a negative light, you might easily conclude that rejecting money is the right way to live. While I certainly believe that greed and the insatiable pursuit of wealth are not healthy attitudes, I also caution you to avoid glorifying poverty. Your core beliefs might have you equating money with greed, but greed is an internal attitude. Money can illuminate greed that already exists, but it does not produce it out of nowhere. If you are afraid of becoming greedy or corrupt, avoiding money is not the answer. Living without financial security has a slew of negative effects on the body and mind, and so I urge you to resist the temptation to reject money in an attempt to avoid greed. That strategy comes from stories that tell us that money corrupts, and from a fear of being tarnished by it. The reality of living with financial insecurity is far darker than these stories let on.

The Big Idea

Financial insecurity harms the mind and body in many ways. Stress, health problems, relationship strain, and exposure to more pollutants and fewer healthy resources are all associated with financial lack. In addition to the physical and emotional difficulties that face those with low income, the social pressures that negative stereotypes create can become a self-fulfilling prophecy that leads to lower performance in academic and professional arenas.

Underlying Factors

Stress It should surprise no one that not having enough money is stressful. What may surprise you is how many people are feeling this stress, and how much it can damage a person's health and behavior.

Each year, the American Psychological Association (APA) publishes *Stress in America: Paying with Our Health*,[1] which reports on the results of a national survey about the causes and levels of stress among Americans. In 2015, the APA said that, "Regardless of the economic climate, money and finances have remained the top stressor since our survey began."[2]

The top stressor.

Regardless of economic climate.

In fact, the APA reports that 64 percent of Americans say money is a "significant" source of stress. Another recent study supports this with 62 percent of respondents saying they are losing sleep over their finances.[3] More than one in four people report feeling stressed about money most or all of the time.[4] Look around you. More than half of the people around you are *losing sleep* over financial stress. They won't let on, of course, but people are deeply stressed about money.

I've said it before, but it's worth reiterating: Financial stress is survival stress, and we pay for this stress with our health. The effect of chronic stress on the body can be devastating. According to the Mayo Clinic, chronic stress puts you at risk for anxiety, depression, heart disease, digestive issues, sleep problems, weight gain, and impairment of mental functions like memory and concentration.[5] Stress is a silent killer, and money is the top source of stress, so we should take this issue very, very seriously.

Money problems bring stress, but what's worse is that money problems also keep people from going to the doctor to get help for the health issues that stress creates. More than one in eight Americans are skipping the doctor when they need medical care because of the cost, and nearly as many have considered it.[6] Add to this the fact that when low-income people do go to the doctor, they often don't get the same quality of care,[7] and the picture looks even bleaker. Inferior medical care means that low-income people effectively pay a higher rate for a lower-quality product[8] than their wealthier neighbors. If people with little to spare take out loans or use credit to pay for medical bills, the additional interest due adds to their financial troubles, and the negative cycle continues.

Stress isn't the only health risk that people face when money is scarce. Have you ever wondered why some people seem stuck in a bad place, unable to "pull themselves up" and better their situation? The ugly truth is that there are many places, even in America, where people face enormous challenges if they want to climb the economic ladder. For example, low-income neighborhoods are often close to heavily polluting industrial sites, leading to increased levels of asthma, cancer, and other diseases.[9] Poorer neighborhoods also tend to have more fast-food restaurants and fewer grocery stores and recreational facilities, contributing to higher obesity rates.[10] The negative feedback loop of financial problems leading to health problems, which lead to financial problems, is just one example of how societal factors related to money can contribute to what are known as *poverty traps.*[11]

Depression On top of the physical effects, there are emotional and mental costs to living with lack that can create another negative feedback loop. Financial stress and unemployment can lead to depression,[12] and people with major depressive disorder often have more difficulty managing their finances. As psychologist and author Richard Zwolinski puts it, "If feelings of despair and feelings that nothing matters prevail, why pay the bills? This can lead to credit problems, utility shutdowns, eviction, job loss, fines, and even jail."[13] Financial trouble leads to depression, which increases financial trouble—another negative feedback loop.

Relationship Strain Another obvious but important finding is that money stress can create relationship difficulties. In fact, arguments about money are the top predictor of divorce, according to Dr. Sonya Britt of Kansas State University.[14] She also notes that couples' arguments about money tend to be longer, more intense, and involve harsher language than other types of arguments. Apparently, when we fight about money, we tend to get nasty. While some research puts money issues a bit lower down on the list of reasons for divorce (e.g., an Institute for Divorce Financial Analysts study placed it at number three[15]), money has historically been a leading cause of marital strife. Again, this probably surprises no one, but it's worth a mention since it means that money problems can potentially hurt our most important relationships.

When it comes to the rest of the family, it seems that growing up poor can have lasting health effects on children. One famous study involving nearly two million people in Sweden found that kids who grew up in homes where the head of the household was a manual laborer had a lower life expectancy than those whose parents held higher-status (and higher-paying) jobs, regardless of their income and education levels in adulthood.[16] Subsequent studies saw similar results with Korean[17] and British[18] subjects. This means that kids whose parents are physical laborers are more likely to get sick or die young than children of higher-income parents, even if those kids grow up to earn high incomes themselves. This leads to all sorts of questions, the most obvious being . . . why?

Some researchers explain the lower life expectancy by pointing out that kids in low-income households are more often exposed to things like noise pollution, lead paint, and tobacco smoke at key points in their development.[19] All of these can lead to illness or developmental problems. Other scientists say that kids who grow up in poverty often don't have consistent exposure to the things they need for healthy emotional and social development:

> Low-income parents are often overwhelmed by diminished self-esteem, depression, and a sense of powerlessness and inability to cope—feelings that may get passed along to their children in the form of insufficient nurturing, negativity, and a general failure to focus on children's needs. In a study of emotional problems of children of single mothers, Keegan-Eamon and Zuehl (2001) found that the stress of poverty increases depression rates among mothers, which results in an increased use of physical punishment. Children themselves are also susceptible to depression: research shows that poverty is a major predictor of teenage depression (Denny, Clark, Fleming, & Wall, 2004).
> —Eric Jensen, *Teaching with Poverty in Mind* (2009)[20]

Dr. Jensen paints a pretty dark picture of what growing up in a low-income home can be like for both parents and kids. Sure, financial stress can lead to some huge problems, but not *all* low-income people are living in polluted neighborhoods or facing lots of relationship issues. What about people who grow up in modest but otherwise healthy homes with supportive family relationships and no emotional or cognitive deficits to speak of? Is lack of money still an issue, psychologically speaking?

The Threat of Judgment Several studies have been done in various countries that asked people to perform certain intellectual tasks. When the tasks were described as tests of intellectual ability, people from lower-income backgrounds performed worse than people from more affluent families. On the other hand, when the *same tasks* were described as being unrelated to intellectual ability, there was no difference in performance between the low-income and the affluent participants.[21] Why would the description of certain tasks change how people from low-income backgrounds perform on them? The researchers who conducted these studies believe the difference has to do with what social psychologists call *stereotype threat*.

When you feel afraid that others might judge you because of negative stereotypes, that's stereotype threat. Anyone who belongs to a group that is stigmatized in some way, be it a racial minority, an economic class, a gender, sexual orientation, or something else, is subject to stereotype threat. For example, there is a myth that women aren't as good at math as men. When women are reminded of this stereotype before a difficult math test, they *do* perform worse than the men, but they also score lower than the women who are not reminded of the gender stereotype.[22] There is also a myth that blacks don't do as well as whites on standardized tests. When race is emphasized before the test, the stereotype is supported, but when race is not mentioned, blacks tend to perform as well *or better than* their white peers.[23]

We see the effects of stereotype threat all over. Researchers have been able to measure it when the elderly are given memory tasks,[24] when women are given driving tests,[25] and when gay men are taking care of children.[26] In all of these instances, reminding people of negative biases made them do worse at the task. My favorite study among them put women in a driving simulation. In this study, the researchers found that reminding women of the negative stereotypes about female drivers made them significantly more likely to run over digital pedestrians.[27]

Is stereotype threat really such a big problem for people who grew up in lower-income households? After all, our movies and fairy tales often glorify the poor, so maybe there really isn't much of a stigma, right? Unfortunately, on the whole, social psychologists have found that people from all income groups seem to hold negative biases about the poor. Dr. Ryan Pickering is an assistant professor of psychology at Allegheny College. His research focuses on the various effects of socio-economic status (SES), and he has spent years researching these social biases. In a review of the research on stereotypes about low-income people, Dr. Pickering noted the following:

Researchers have shown that the poor are labeled as uneducated, lazy, criminal, stupid, immoral, and violent (Chafel, 1997; Cozzarelli, Wilkenson, & Tagler, 2001; Hoyt, 1999). One study found that middle-class students rated lower class women as more dirty, hostile, confused, illogical, impulsive, incoherent, irresponsible, inconsiderate, and superstitious than their higher-class counterparts (Cyrus, 1997). Individuals living in, or close to, poverty are frequently misrepresented by cultural stereotypes, including the "white trash" stereotype. In the United States, the "white trash" stereotype presents lower-SES whites as stupid, coarse, violent, dirty, and sexually unrestrained (Spencer & Castano, 2007; Wray, 2006). A study by Loughnan, Haslam, Sutton, and Spencer (2013) found that the "white trash" stereotype is also characterized by the "infrahumanization effect" (Leyens et al., 2000), or a representation of individuals as less human/more bestial, with a lower capacity to experience human emotions.

There is also a consistent view from higher classes that the poor are personally responsible for their plight (Chafel, 1997). Interestingly, and contrary to what one might expect, these negative attitudes toward the poor have been found to increase as level of education increases (Brantlinger, 2003; Jackman & Muha, 1984).[28]

The strain of stereotype threat on mental resources (brain drain) means that the poor have to work harder, mentally and psychologically, to perform at the same level as their nonstereotyped peers. What's more, we can be biased against *ourselves*, effectively causing our own chronic stress. In a fascinating study published in 2013, researchers found that people who identified as low-income and also had negative biases about the poor had higher levels of inflammatory markers in their body, putting them at higher risk for health problems. In other words, if you grew up in a lower-income home, and you have any biases against the poor, then you may be subjecting *yourself* to stereotype threat, and that self-judgment (or fear of it) can lead to health problems.[29] If there were ever a case for treating yourself with kindness, this is one.

Okay, but some people are going to work harder under the threat of judgment in order to prove the bias wrong, right? If you think that the threat of judgment would motivate a person to do better in order to prove the stereotype wrong, you're certainly not alone. In one study of gender stereotypes on math tests, researchers asked a group of men *and* women how they thought the stereotype of women being bad at math would affect the women taking the test. Both men and women assumed that the women taking the test would work harder and out-perform the men in order to prove the stereotype wrong, but this is not what happened.[30] As it turns out, trying to prove the stigma wrong might actually be the reason that people under the threat of judgment perform *worse.*

While we still don't know exactly why stereotype threat lowers performance so consistently, most researchers involved in this work believe that the increased levels of anxiety and psychological arousal from trying to combat the stereotype may act as a drain on precious cognitive resources, leading to lower performance. In other words, by trying to prove the bias wrong, we use up a lot of brainpower that otherwise we would be putting toward the task at hand.

Have you ever had to take a difficult test and spent so much time looking at the clock and worrying that you wouldn't finish in time that it took your attention away from the test itself? It's the same thing with stereotype threat. The fear of judgment wastes precious mental energy, and bias becomes a self-fulfilling prophecy.

Defense Mechanisms Stereotype threat has other negative consequences on mental health as well. For example, to explain lower performance on difficult tasks, we often attribute failure to internal weaknesses and become very self-critical. Instead of seeing the anxiety of stereotype threat as the real cause of poor performance, we (women more often than men) blame ourselves for our failures.[31] Assuming that you are inadequate, rather than recognizing that the fear of judgment causes brain drain, can be a very effective way of undermining your confidence and self-esteem.

Another way we can sabotage our own success is through *self-handicapping.* This is where a person finds possible reasons for failing before they even try a task in order to make failure easier to explain if it happens. We tell ourselves we probably won't get that raise because there is a recession, or because Janet in Accounting doesn't like us, and then we won't feel as bad if we don't get it. Or, we might employ *task discounting,* where we belittle the task in the first place so that failure won't hurt as much. "College isn't that important, anyway," we say to ourselves. Then, we fail to advocate for ourselves or put our all into the applications. The fear of failure can lead to failure in the same way that the fear of judgment can be self-fulfilling.

More extreme defense mechanisms against failure or judgment include distancing ourselves from the social group under threat, or even a complete disassociation from the group. We try to avoid being judged by deciding that we don't *really* belong to the group that's being judged. While these tactics may reduce the pain of failure or rejection, they can cause terrible social and emotional pain, and all of them ignore the true problem: that the effort involved in combatting the stereotypes by which we fear being judged drains our resources.

Another damaging effect of stereotype threat is that many people who fear being cast in a negative light by prejudice will simply avoid situations or environments where they think they might be judged. This is a natural response to the fear of judgment, but since people from low-SES backgrounds can feel judged in academic, work, and social environments, that means they'd be avoiding many, many situations. Remember the boy on the bus? He avoided having kids from school come home to play because of stereotype threat. He will never know how many friendships, opportunities, and joys he passed up because of the social anxiety that stereotype threat caused him in grade school. Fear of judgment can keep us from networking, sticking our neck out for a promotion, or applying for college or a dream job. In the long run, all of this can have a big impact on our bottom line.

Social Shaming What about when someone starts to climb up the socioeconomic ladder? Surely their friends and family will all support them, right? Not always. In addition to being judged by the more affluent, people in low-income communities can also face heavy peer pressure to *stay* low-income. Our society has what Dr. James Grubman, owner of FamilyWealth Consulting, calls a "hostile envy" of the rich. That hostility is often expressed through the social rejection of people with higher incomes.

In a powerful 2009 article published on PsychologyToday.com, Dr. Ted Klontz, coauthor of *Mind over Money*, talked about his own experiences growing up in a home where his rich uncle was vilified by other family members. Because of his family's core beliefs about money, it was simply assumed that the uncle's wealth came from exploiting other people. Dr. Klontz said the experience made a deep impression. "The unstated message was, if you want to be thrown out of the family, be successful like him."[32] Dr. Klontz is not alone. Many of us are steeped in social environments that criticize and shame the wealthy. To be upwardly mobile in that kind of setting is a form of social suicide. This kind of social pressure often creates a choice between being financially secure and lonely, or struggling in poverty, but at least being among friends.

One way to get around this is what Dr. Pickering describes as "code-switching." Code-switching describes a shift in language depending on your environment. One person told me about his experience of having to change his speech in order to avoid getting made fun of by his family after he went away to college. "When I go home," he said, "I have to switch to my Maine accent. 'She says she ain't goin' to thah stowah.' 'I don't know whether I's goin' or not.' 'Did you heah 'bout them folks from Chiner?' If I don't, my language use is criticized. My sister asked my brother once, 'Why doesn't he talk like us?' before I figured this out."

It's also common for minority college students from poor backgrounds to "talk white" at school, and use Ebonics or Spanglish at home. Code-switching is one way of coping with social pressures, but it casts light on how people who try to move up the economic ladder have to consider the relationship costs involved.

Clearly, people with low incomes face many challenges. We have seen that financial strain can lead to increased stress, health risks, relationship stress, and lower performance on tasks that are relevant to education and career advancement. This doesn't mean that people with low incomes are necessarily less happy or fulfilled in life, but it does mean that there are challenges that need to be overcome if a person with modest resources wants to thrive, psychologically. On top of this, if someone aims to move up the ladder, they may face difficult social challenges along the way.

What to Do about It

First, take stock. Whether you think of yourself as rich, poor, or somewhere in between, ask yourself:

- What situations do I avoid or fear because of money?
- Do I ever feel worried that people will judge me negatively due to my social, economic, gender, or racial group? How has this affected my views or behavior?
- Do I personally experience any of the effects of chronic financial stress?
- Am I receiving adequate medical care, or have I avoided the doctor due to the cost?
- Do I fear that if I were to focus on building up my financial strength, I might lose friends, or be judged by my loved ones?

Get LOADED   If you want to reduce the negative impacts of financial strain in your own life, you can work by managing the symptoms (e.g., stress relief techniques) or by removing the cause (creating more financial security with the resources you have). I recommend a combination of the two. The money management technique laid out later in this book (Chapter 4, "The LOADED Budget") can help you to learn how to make the most of your personal resources and meet more of your needs. Financial change doesn't happen overnight, though; in the meantime, while you are building a stronger financial life, you can also work to reduce the negative effects of stereotype threat and stress on your own psyche.

Get Calm   There is no need to lay out stress relief techniques here, as there are millions of free resources available to teach how to find calm in life's storms. Breathing exercises, meditation, spiritual practice, exercise, healthy eating, talk therapy, and medications all can be very effective means of reducing stress. What may be the most important step is recognizing that your financial stress is worthy of your attention, and that taking action to find peace is worth your time. There is a bit more about how to promote positive emotional experiences with your money and reduce negative ones a little further on as well. Reducing the effects of stress on your mind and body may also help improve the quality of your relationships and reduce conflict in that area of your life.

Get Affirmed When it comes to stereotype threat, you can try affirmations. I was skeptical about the effectiveness of affirmations for a long time, but carefully orchestrated scientific work in this area shows clearly that writing about your core values reduces the effects of stereotype threat.[33] When you take a moment to think about the things that really matter to you, suddenly the perceptions of others just don't seem to hold as much sway. Using affirmations in this context is easy. Just take a few minutes (right now if you like) to write down a couple of things that you really care about and value. For example, "I deeply appreciate honesty" or "Being caring and compassionate are my deepest values." Researchers have found that thinking about our values like this can have a long-lasting positive effect on our behaviors. The next time you feel afraid of judgment, pull out those few sentences and read them to yourself.

Privilege: Why Having an Advantage Is Great . . . and Not So Great

We've talked about how not having money can create problems, but what about having lots of money? On the surface, it would seem that people with wealth must be free from any psychological difficulty associated with money. After all, they are not losing sleep over unpaid bills or avoiding the doctor when they have a health problem. They are not judged as lazy, dirty, or ignorant, and so they must be free from all the negative effects of money or lack. This is absolutely not true. Wealth and privilege have their own suite of psychological consequences, and the rich face negative prejudice as well as the poor. The caricatures of Scrooge and Mr. Burns paint the rich as greedy and exploitative monsters, but do they reflect real life? Are the rich truly less compassionate than the poor? To answer these questions, we will look at a few studies of how money and privilege affect human behavior.

The Big Idea

Money appears to affect our psychology in several ways. First, if we were raised in middle- and upper-income homes, we tend to have more personal choice and control over our lives due to fewer constraints on resources, and fewer of the environmental limitations mentioned in the previous section on lack. We didn't live in neighborhoods with as much pollution, and we had access to better food and recreation options. The benefits of privilege seem to lead to greater feelings of personal power, and Western culture definitely encourages independence rather than interdependence.[34] These factors can lead to a strong sense of personal agency and control over one's destiny. In other words, people who grow up in higher-income homes tend to feel a stronger sense of control over their lives than people from lower-income homes.

So far so good—empowerment is great! But what about when people have a real advantage over others? Some research shows that having privilege affects the way we treat others as well as the way we think about our own abilities. On top of this, just thinking about money leads to better intellectual performance and higher levels of self-reliance in laboratory studies, but it also appears to lessen people's willingness to help others.

Underlying Factors

Interestingly, in studies where students have been put into scenarios where they are given a *clear and unfair* advantage over others, they will often still claim responsibility for coming out on top. One famous study by Dr. Paul Piff of the University of California at Berkeley paired students in a short version of Monopoly where the rules were very obviously skewed in one person's favor. This favored player was given more money at the outset, and other more subtle advantages along the way (like getting to roll two dice instead of just one on every turn). The privileged players tended to grow louder and more aggressive as the game went on, and even helped themselves to more of the snacks than their disadvantaged opponent. Even though at the beginning of the game, the privileged people often commented on how unfairly advantaged they were, when asked afterward why they won, they tended to attribute their success to their game-playing skills and decision making.[35] These players knew that they were given a huge advantage, yet they still believed that their win was due to skill and personal effort. They conveniently forgot the advantages they were given, and felt sure that their decisions were to be thanked for their win. Why does this matter? Because it demonstrates how our minds cope with privilege—apparently, by denying it exists.

The problem with privilege is that it's blind. One of the greatest forms of privilege is the privilege not to know you are privileged! If that sounds like doublespeak, consider this: As a woman, I am very aware of the disadvantages I might face with regard to equal treatment in the workplace, the mathematics classroom, and the mechanic's shop. On the other hand, I can easily forget that I am a *white* woman, an American citizen, and well educated. I am privileged as well as disadvantaged, but which do you think is more obvious to me in my day-to-day life? I am far more aware of the efforts I make to succeed than the advantages I'm afforded along the way. I think privilege is blind because it's usually experienced as a *lack of barriers* rather than the presence of favoritism. We make an effort, and we aren't blocked, so we feel that our effort led to success, when this is only part of the story. In one sense, having privilege is great! It means you don't face barriers everywhere you turn. The trouble comes when we think that everyone else has the same situation. To work hard and succeed is wonderful. To then turn around and tell someone else who faces a type of discrimination we don't to "just do what I did" is not helpful. If they could, they would. When we are the beneficiaries of privilege, whether it is in the form of wealth, opportunities, physical talents, access to education, social connections, or anything else, we can very easily forget that we have advantages that others don't. This can lead us to judge others as incompetent rather than understanding that the path they are walking is made of very different terrain.

Getting back to the research, while Dr. Piff's studies are interesting, and they certainly make headlines due to articles with titles like "Does Money Make You Mean?," it is hard to say that the way a person behaves in a cute and inconsequential situation like a rigged Monopoly game is really indicative of how true privilege affects behavior. Still, there are many studies in this line of research that show a link between privilege and what's known as *system justification*.

We Want to Believe That the World Is Fair We are all looking for meaning in the complex and sometimes chaotic world around us, and when we are the beneficiary of privilege due to chance or a fluke of history, we have a few ways to interpret our situation. We can chalk it all up to random chance, in which case we might be forced to wrestle with feelings of guilt (because equally deserving others do not have the same privilege) or anxiety (because we may become a target for theft, cons, or violence). Second, we can decide that the system is unfair, and face the feelings of guilt and anxiety that accompany being the beneficiaries of an unfair advantage. Last, we can decide that the system is fundamentally fair, meaning that somehow we must be deserving of that privilege. That way we can enjoy our situation and not have to feel guilty or anxious.

Which do you think you would choose? If people who are given an advantage in a game with no real-world consequences end up taking credit for their winnings, and tell themselves that they deserved to win, then it's pretty likely that people who have an advantage in real-world scenarios are even more prone to do so. Very few of us *want* to exploit others or benefit at their expense. It is far easier on our psyches to trust that the system is fundamentally fair so we don't have to feel guilty for our lot in life. Many faith traditions teach that there is an underlying order and justice to the world around us, which can contribute to this tendency to justify unfair systems. I do not believe this makes us "mean." This is all very human and not indicative of cruelty at all. In fact, the very reason we engage in system justification is because we *want* to believe that the world is fair. The more we believe in an innately just world, the more difficult it is to reconcile extreme inequality with our worldview, unless we conclude that, somehow, inequality is deserved. It's a coping strategy, not a personal failure.

MoneyThink There's another reason why people who have more money may appear to be less compassionate or willing to help those less fortunate, and again, it has nothing to do with being "mean."

As it turns out, just thinking about money has both positive and negative effects on people's behaviors. Thinking about money makes people work harder at challenging tasks, try on their own longer before asking for help, generally do better on intellectual tasks, and prefer to work alone.[36] It would appear that money triggers an independent and achievement-focused state of mind. Maybe the next time you have to take a test or finish a big project, you should think about dollar bills first?

On the other hand, this independence has a downside. Not only does thinking about money make us want to be self-reliant, it also makes us dislike having others depend on us. Thinking about money induces a state of mind where we are more achievement oriented, but less likely to help others or desire for them to want our help. What's more, the effect still appears when people don't know that they are thinking about money. Even very subtle reminders of money can change people's mental focus to an independent, achievement-oriented mind-set.

How do researchers know when someone is thinking about money in an unconscious way? They purposely give money reminders to one group, and not to another. For example, in one study, people were split randomly into groups and given a word-unscrambling task. In this task, each person was presented with 30 sets of five words each, and they needed to use four of the five to make a phrase. The task was simple enough, and nobody had a clue that the researchers wanted to get some of them thinking about money. Here's the clever part: The people in the control group were given neutral words like "cold it desk outside is," which would become "it is cold outside." In the second group, half of the scrambled word groups had money references such as "high a salary desk paying," which would become "a high paying salary." These people were not aware that they were being primed to think about money. (If you're skeptical about that, the researchers asked them later to confirm.) After the word task, everyone was given another challenging but solvable task to complete. As expected, the people who had been shown money words worked longer on their own before asking for help than the control group.[37] This tendency to prefer independent achievement when thinking about money has been repeated in many other studies, with consistent results.

In Poland, Dr. Agata Gasiorowska and her colleagues have been conducting research into how interacting with money affects the behavior of children. They performed a study on children who were old enough to know what coins were and how money is used, but too young to have much of a concept past the idea that the coins had value associated with them, and that money is used to buy things.

They randomly separated the kids into two groups. In the control group, each child was given a handful of buttons that varied in size, shape, and color, and was allowed to play with them for a couple of minutes. The other group played with coins. Once the task was completed, each child was taken to a second testing room and given a very challenging labyrinth. They were told to find their way through with a pencil, but also that they could stop or ask for help at any time. The researchers found that the kids who played with the coins were more persistent in attempting the labyrinth, and they were more likely to complete it correctly than the children who played with buttons.[38]

In another study, children were again given either coins or buttons to play with, and then taken to a second room. This time, instead of a labyrinth, they found a researcher who was readying the room for another study. The researcher asked the child if he or she would help to get the room prepared by helping to pick up crayons. The kids who had been playing with money collected fewer crayons, on average, than those who had played with buttons.[39] Apparently even kids become more diligent, and less helpful, when they think about money.

It is too early in this field of work to be sure why we have this response to thinking about money, but after many repeated studies, we can be fairly certain that the effect of thinking about money on our behavior is real.

I like to call this state of mind "MoneyThink." It is important to be clear that when a person is operating under the influence of Money-Think, they are *not* necessarily thinking about money consciously. Rather, MoneyThink refers to the state of increased desire to accomplish challenging tasks independently, and to be free from the burdens of having others depend upon you for help. In the studies that have been done to date, it seems that MoneyThink increases people's desire to achieve;

they perform better on challenging tasks, and they work harder and are more persistent than when MoneyThink is not activated. There are clear, positive benefits to persistence, independence, and achievement.

What seems to be the downside is that MoneyThink also creates a desire to work alone and to have others be independent (not needing help) as well, which from a social perspective can be taken as cold, uncaring, or antisocial. What does any of this have to do with our day-to-day lives? The phenomenon of MoneyThink plays right into our negative cultural stereotypes about the rich being cold-hearted and mean, unwilling to help, and concerned only with getting richer. I want to raise a warning flag about those stereotypes here. Rather than interpret the antisocial behavior that sometimes accompanies money and wealth as meanness, let's look at MoneyThink from a cultural perspective. It is very possible that what some see as a lack of compassion or caring is actually a sign of a social orientation that values self-reliance over interdependence.

The Paradox It would appear that money creates a catch-22: If you don't have it, your performance suffers, your relationships suffer, and your life expectancy drops. But if you have it, you may be more likely to engage in system justification or MoneyThink. Do our experiences with poverty and privilege have to be like this? Isn't there a middle way?

Thankfully, the answer is yes. If you are hoping to become more financially secure, yet you want to hold on to your values of compassion and social interconnectedness, there is good news. While the influence of MoneyThink is real, as it turns out there are some very simple things a person can do that completely eliminate the effects of MoneyThink on behavior.

What to Do about It

Again, we want to first take stock. Ask yourself the following questions:

- ► What do I value more, relationships or achievement?
- ► Does it bother me when people ask for my help? If so, why? Does their reliance on me conflict with my values?

► What reactions have I personally received when I have relied on others? Was I ever criticized or punished for needing help?
► How do I think that my upbringing has shaped my work ethic and my view of relationships?
► Are these views serving me well today?

If the prospect of MoneyThink concerns you, and you want to be sure to maintain your interpersonal values even as you grow in financial wealth, take heart. There are a few very simple activities that have been shown to completely eliminate the effects of MoneyThink. Here is a short list of simple things you can do that may help you to avoid the negative effects of MoneyThink:

► **Write about equality.** In one study, researchers found that having people write three ways in which other people were equal to them significantly reduced the negative effects of entitlement.[40]
► **Commune with nature.** Several studies conducted at the University of California at Berkeley found that looking at beautiful nature photos led to more generosity and trust among participants. Also, when study subjects were seated in a lab with beautiful plants, they showed more helpful behavior than the subjects who were not around beautiful plants.[41]
► **Get in touch with awe.** Dr. Piff and his colleagues found that when people simply remembered a natural scene that had filled them with awe in the past, it triggered a sense of what they called the "small self." This sense of smallness in a vast universe then increased generosity and ethical behavior in the tasks that followed.[42] So, if you think your ego might be getting a little inflated, getting awed can bring you back down to size.
► **Train in compassion.** The connection between lower-income individuals and prosocial behaviors may be linked to egalitarian values, specifically putting a high value on having compassion for others.[43] If you want to increase your capacity for compassion, you are in luck. Research has shown that compassion can be trained and developed through simple meditation practices such as loving-kindness

meditation (LKM). Compassion meditation does not have to be linked to a spiritual practice. Several types of secular compassion meditation have been developed. LKM is one that can easily be practiced with no religious or spiritual elements involved.

A growing body of evidence has shown that compassion can be increased intentionally and that this is associated with significant reduction in negative affect, increase in positive affect, reduced chronic pain, and increased feelings of social connection and positivity toward strangers.

—Dr. Thomas Plante[44]

Prejudice—We've All Got It

Cultural differences between income groups can contribute to stereotyping and prejudice. To be fair, most of the stereotypes about the wealthy are positive. Studies show that people tend to view the wealthy as more friendly, competent, and likable than the poor. Yet there is still a very negative undercurrent to attitudes about wealth in many circles. Some view the wealthy as successful and competent, but others view the same people as greedy and uncaring. The hostile envy that Dr. Grubman speaks of is apparent in many of the subtle judgments of our language. For example, what is the difference between someone who is "fabulously wealthy" and someone who is "filthy, stinking rich?" The difference is in the attitude of the person making the judgment, and that attitude is born from culture, values, and core beliefs.

The Big Idea

Most of us don't think of ourselves as rich or poor, but somewhere in the middle. Still, regardless of how we self-identify, we tend to think in terms of "us" and "them," and this is certainly true when it comes to income classes. This natural human tendency creates a large social divide, and makes it easy to fall prey to simplistic biases and judgments. Those judgments not only hurt our ability to relate to people outside our own income group, but can also serve as barriers to economic mobility and lead to financial self-sabotage.

Underlying Factors

Going back to cultural stories for a moment, let's consider recent books like *The Hunger Games* series and movies like *In Time*. In these stories, society is divided into several sections, with the extremely wealthy living in one area and the impoverished in another. Physical walls separate each social class in these fictional societies from the others, and people live their lives in isolation from those in different circumstances. This isolation and division eventually leads to rebellion and revolution.

I see these stories as powerful, cautionary tales. Our own society has no walls dividing people according to their incomes. Still, how often do we socialize with those who have dramatically different economic lives? We don't *need* walls because we create them ourselves through the simple human tendency to hang out with people similar to us. While this may be a normal way to socialize, it creates an environment where it is easy to dehumanize people that we see as "others." This gives rise to biases that get woven into our personal narratives.

Social Orientation The divide between socioeconomic groups in America has to do with more than just money. There are cultural distinctions that separate us as well (they're not called *socio*economic groups for nothing). Many people paint the entire American culture with the broad brush of "independence," as if we all value self-reliance the same. America, and Western cultures in general, are characterized as valuing independence. In contrast, Eastern cultures have a foundational belief in interdependence. However, when we compare the beliefs and attitudes of people with high and low incomes in America, there is a stark contrast between them. In low-income communities, people often need to rely on one another, and a culture that values interdependence and social capital has evolved out of this need. Due in part to the common experience of struggle, the low-income culture puts a heavy emphasis on family, loyalty, cooperation, and friendship. Depending on one another, and being a part of a larger whole that one contributes to and leans on in times of need, are common values in this culture, and they more closely resemble Eastern societies than the independent American stereotype.

In one study of people from America (labeled as an independent society) and Russia (labeled as an interdependent society), the researchers found that in both countries, the people from lower income backgrounds had more interdependent self-views than those with higher incomes. In other words, even in a culture that values independence as much as America does, if you grow up in a low-income environment, you are more likely to identify with a more interdependent culture. But, what does it mean to "identify with an interdependent culture" rather than valuing independence? Think of it this way: In an independent society, "the squeaky wheel gets the grease," but in an interdependent society, "a stake that sticks out will be hammered." In one culture, standing out from the crowd is praised and rewarded. In the other, standing out invites criticism. Independent cultures view originality, self-reliance, and autonomy as highly positive traits. The more a person is able to make his own way, the better, and the courage to defy tradition is highly praised. We see this theme in many of our cultural stories. Rags-to-riches stories are one example, but any tale of revolution, iconoclasm, or standing against the crowd for a higher ideal plays well to people from an independent society.

On the other hand, groups that are based on interdependence are less wowed by individualism, and more impressed by acts of service, caring, and loyalty. Military groups are one example of an interdependent society. When you and your neighbor rely on one another for survival, standing out from the crowd is less important than being a part of the team. An interdependent society survives through cooperation and solidarity with one another. "All for one, and one for all" is the motto of an interdependent society. Standing out can be seen as an act of defiance, or lack of commitment to the needs of the group. In an interdependent culture, the needs of the many outweigh the needs of the few, and to stand out can invite harsh criticism.

Depending on which type of social orientation you received in your formative years, you will likely have developed a few core beliefs about how a person should behave with respect to family, friends, and neighbors. If you were raised in an interdependent group, then family and community are more likely to hold a high priority for you and your peers. If you were raised in a group that valued independence, then leadership, self-reliance, and achievement are likely to be more important to you and to the people who you care about. In one group, a person gains respect and friendship by helping others. In the other, a person gains respect and friendship by helping themselves and *not* relying on others. It is not hard to see, then, how people from one social orientation or the other could view the other group in a negative light. To the independent-minded, those with interdependent beliefs appear to lack ambition, vision, and work ethic, and care too much about what other people think and feel. From the interdependent view, self-reliant people lack in compassion, empathy, and helpfulness, and are overly concerned with status and power.

Now consider the effect that money has on the mind, and it is not at all difficult to see why the social expectations of high earners would be focused on achievement and self-reliance. Add to that the fact that people with fewer resources often need to depend on one another for survival, and you can see why an interdependent social system would thrive among them. The cultural clash that results is not only about inequality and the distribution of wealth, but also a conflict of deep values. Perhaps by understanding our differences in the light of social pressures rather than viewing the behavior of others as indicative of personal failings, we can better understand the challenges and strengths of each way of living.

Social psychologists have seen a strong pattern of in-group favoritism (meaning we prefer "us" to "them") that also contributes to class divisions and the demonization of people with values and cultures that differ from our own. We have a natural tendency to favor people from our own "tribe" over those from other groups. If you identify very strongly with your particular socioeconomic group, the effects of social customs and group identification may be particularly strong. If you were raised to value independence, your knee-jerk reaction to watching a store clerk chat with a friend may be to label them as lazy. It may help you to remember that in some cultures time and friendship are the most valuable currency, and that social transaction is not a meaningless activity. On the other hand, if you were raised to value relationships over achievement, you may struggle to keep from judging the ambitious as cold-hearted. Before you make that judgment, try to remind yourself that in some cultures acceptance is won through self-reliance. Be wary of any bias that reduces people to caricatures and groups to labels like "greedy" or "lazy" or "dumb." Those biases can interfere with your own decisions, and sabotage your best efforts to live a healthy and happy financial life.

To assume the poor are lazy, dirty, unambitious, and ignorant is to judge a huge and diverse population by the worst qualities of a few members. Likewise, to judge the poor as more noble, pure-hearted, and generous than the wealthy is to buy into the stereotypes painted by movies and fairy tales, and again judge the whole group based on the qualities of a few. Moreover, the behaviors that contribute to the stereotypes may be due in part to cultural values in poor communities that favor cooperation and interdependence over self-reliance. These values lead to behaviors that may not be reflections of people's actual priorities, but simple conformity under peer pressure. On the other hand, assumptions that the wealthy are competent and friendly, or cold-hearted and greedy, are just as simplistic as biases about the poor. Again, the judgments we make are affected by our core beliefs, which are shaped by our backgrounds and experiences, as well as the cultural values of our community, and how they align or conflict with the values of others.

The effects of socioeconomic prejudice can be incredibly damaging. When people view independence and self-reliance as cold-heartedness and greed, they may hold themselves back from creating a stable financial situation for themselves. If your community sees independence as a betrayal of their values, the social cost of going to college or embarking on a high-paying career may be tremendously high. To become self-reliant in such an environment may mean that you lose your support network and are judged as haughty by your peers. Financial success can be social failure in this environment.

On the other hand, if your community values self-reliance over interdependence, it may be easy to belittle and judge those who are more relationship oriented as having less ability or drive. Also, a community that belittles interdependence can become a lonely place if vulnerability and human connection aren't acceptable on any level. You've heard that it's lonely at the top. This can be true in many ways. Extremes on either end of the dependence–independence spectrum can be unhealthy.

What to Do about It

Stereotypes are similar to core beliefs in that they are the one-sentence version of a larger narrative or story. "The poor are lazy" is the "moral" of a story we are telling ourselves based on limited experiences and our particular environment. "The rich are greedy" is another simplification of a much larger narrative. Just as we talked about challenging your core beliefs about money in your own life, you can challenge your core beliefs about how money affects other people. The two techniques mentioned earlier, changing the narrative and finding a counterexample, are effective here as well.

Movin' on Up

Not only can stereotypes and cultural judgments keep us from valuing others appropriately; they can affect our financial and social behavior if we start out in one culture and then migrate to another. The upwardly mobile often face unexpected cultural challenges that are rooted in core beliefs and community values.

When someone manages to move up the socioeconomic ladder, the culture shock can be tremendous. Climbing such a ladder has emotional challenges that most money books don't discuss. The transitions can be incredibly uncomfortable for many people, and adapting to the new social pressures is often a very difficult emotional journey.

The Big Idea

Core beliefs about money, which may be reinforced by the social cultures of interdependence and independence, can also play a role in how a person adapts to wealth if they do not begin life with money or privilege. When a lower- or middle-income family comes into wealth, they are like immigrants arriving in a new land. There is a new culture to navigate, with new rules to learn, and even a new form of language.

Underlying Factors

Scientists who study cross-cultural psychology have identified three coping strategies that immigrants commonly use to adapt to their new surroundings: avoidance, assimilation, and integration. In his insightful book, *Strangers in Paradise: How Families Adapt to Wealth across Generations*,[45] Dr. James Grubman draws on this cross-cultural psychology to teach the importance of healthy integration when a person has acquired wealth. According to Dr. Grubman, people who migrate to the "land of wealth" fall into these same three categories.

Avoidance Many who come into wealth harbor fears that they will lose critical parts of themselves or their heritage if they adopt a wealthy lifestyle. Like immigrants who don't learn the language, hold firmly to their old customs, and rarely associate with the natives of their new country, avoiders cling tightly to their middle-income identity.

Some level of concern for preserving one's values and relationships among the newly wealthy is certainly appropriate, but this can become a problem when people fearfully hide their wealth from the world, and even from their children.

"By and large, the avoidance response is an anxiety-type paradigm," says Dr. Grubman. "Avoiders are constantly asking themselves, 'What if?'" Dr. Grubman explains. "If I spend money, what if they see, and then I am a target for fraud, or loans and gifts? What if I seem like a greedy person? What if I lose my soul when I embrace wealth?"

Avoiding can also lead to family turmoil. Children of avoiders may not learn of their parents' wealth until well into their adult years. This can lead to feelings of hurt and betrayal, especially if they have made major concessions in their life decisions based on the assumption of being limited financially. The second generation is also left to manage a large body of wealth without ever having been taught, or having observed, positive wealth-management skills. Too often, when avoiders die, "fear and money are bundled together tightly and passed on as one inheritance," says Dr. Grubman. As a result, the next generation is likely to lose wealth.

How can you tell if you're an avoider?

1. Do you believe any negative stereotypes about the wealthy?
2. Are you afraid that embracing wealth could make you become like the stereotypes?
3. Do you fear that wealth will make you a target for fraud, scams, or hostile envy from others?

If you answered yes to any of these questions, you might be prone to avoiding.

Assimilation Some immigrants to the United States try to be as American as possible, as quickly as possible. They learn English, eat American food, listen to American music, and generally break ties with the world they left behind. Many who come into wealth do the same.

This strategy of transition makes a clean break from the lower and middle classes, opting to relish the luxuries available in the land of wealth. Many people who assimilate to wealth do not want anyone to know that they come from more humble circumstances.

Where avoiders tend to hold on to their money and never feel safe, assimilators experience an exhilarating sense of safety and freedom—but often spend themselves right back out of wealth.

Like the children of avoiders, the children of assimilators rarely see positive examples of wealth management. The skills that are critical to managing a family's wealth across generations (such as weighing a purchase against one's budget) are lost on assimilators. An assimilator may wonder why anyone with millions of dollars would bother with a budget.

How can you tell if you're an assimilator?

1. Do you believe that money is a sign of success, power, or prestige?
2. Does the idea of wealth arouse feelings of powerful desire?

3. Do you try to avoid people finding out about your more humble past?

If you answered yes to any of these questions, you might be prone to assimilating.

Integration Integration is the best—and most challenging—strategy for transitioning to a life of wealth. Integration involves maintaining the values and skills from the middle class that are the most useful and treasured, while remaining open to learning new ways of living that are unique to wealth.

Integrators talk openly with their children about their wealth and involve them in financial decisions. Integrators want to learn the financial skills that are necessary to managing wealth and model them for their children regularly. Integrators generally feel a sense of peaceful continuity between the land they left behind and the land to which they have come. They focus on helping their children understand how to enjoy wealth while keeping the important values from the middle class alive in their home.

How can you tell if you're an integrator?

1. Do you put little stock in stereotypes about the wealthy (whether positive or negative)?
2. Does the idea of wealth trigger a fairly minor emotional response?
3. Do you feel a sense of continuity between your past and present, embracing your new life while also holding on to the values and people you care about from your past?

If you answered yes to any of these questions, you may be able to integrate well.

What to Do about It

The three strategies are not mutually exclusive. You may find yourself moving in and out of each strategy over time. Ideally, you will settle into a life where the parts of your past that you value most are well integrated with the parts of your new life that bring you joy and security. To get there, you may need to break yourself out of avoiding or assimilating from time to time.

According to Dr. Grubman, the things that help avoiders are the same things that help people with anxiety. No amount of financial security can help with avoidance because "the problem isn't the money—it's the 'What-ifs,'" says Grubman. "The trick for avoiders is to turn the 'What if?' into a 'So what?'" He suggests that avoiders challenge themselves to spend a bit more in order to see that the land of wealth may, in fact, be a safer place than they believe.

Assimilators need to learn to enjoy the benefits of wealth while exercising moderation. Identifying activities and things unrelated to money that bring you joy can be a good start. Learning about money management and modeling moderation for your children will go a long way to helping them maintain wealth. There are plenty of resources available for people who are transitioning to great wealth. Dr. Grubman's book, *Strangers in Paradise*, and the Sudden Money Institute website are good places to start.

Money and Cognitive Psychology: How Specific Thinking Patterns Affect Financial Decisions

For many of us, the greatest challenge we face is not in confronting the social backlash from financial independence, but in changing our habits to reach financial freedom in the first place. Many people struggle to make changes in their financial behaviors even when they want very much to advance their economic situation. Social expectations and challenges aside, several other internal factors of psychology have been shown to affect financial behaviors. Some of these are conscious and some are unconscious. Understanding them can help you to discover if you might be getting in your own way when it comes to financial decisions. Since beginning my journey into the world of financial psychology, I have been particularly interested in how differences in thought patterns affect financial behaviors. Here I will briefly describe a couple of the trends that emerged as I have dug into these topics, as well as a few suggestions about how to use the insights from this research to your benefit.

Why Retail Therapy Feels Good: Identity and Ego Depletion

We live in a consumer culture. Shopping is not just a chore, but often a pastime. Many of us could be saving a lot more if we didn't love shopping so much, but how did buying things become such a big part of our lives? Why is shopping such a pleasurable activity, and how can we learn to spend less without feeling like we're going on a restrictive diet? This section covers some of the ways we use money to meet emotional needs, and how to tackle expensive shopping habits without feeling deprived.

The Big Idea

We shop for fun. We shop to feel better. We shop for social connection. We shop to buy things that help us feel more like the person we want to be. We shop to fulfill our sense of identity.

Underlying Factor: The Possession–Self Link

Shopping takes on a whole new meaning when you understand how our brains incorporate physical objects into our sense of identity. As it happens, our minds don't distinguish between "me" and "mine." In other words, the things that we own get incorporated by our minds into our sense of self, so that who we are includes not only our bodies, minds, and personalities, but also our possessions.[46] This possession–self link is especially strong with items that represent key parts of our personalities or our personal narratives. Think about Kathy and her lost engagement ring. When she lost her ring, she went through the stages of grief. I recently spoke to a man who had to grieve the loss of some treasured family heirlooms in a divorce, and another who said that when his bike was stolen it was like losing a part of himself. This is a very typical response when we experience the loss, theft, or destruction of items that are closely linked to our sense of personal identity.

When you understand how the possession–self link works, it sheds light on many things that might otherwise be confusing. Why, for example, is it often so difficult for the elderly to part with belongings that they have no use for? Why is your grandmother so fixated on making sure that you know every detail of the story behind how her father came by that writing desk before she passes it on? These items are intensely emotionally charged because they hold within them the personal narrative of an entire life – a life that is coming to an end, and the stories are all that will remain. Why do people feel personally violated when someone steals from them?[47] Because a part of themselves has been taken away. Why does shopping feel so good when you've had a really bad day? Because when your identity is bruised or you feel small, you can easily feel more like the person you *want* to be by buying something that fits with that identity.

The fact that we incorporate material objects into our sense of self opens new doors for understanding our relationship with money and the things we own. When I first learned about the possession–self link, it immediately helped me to see why we can so easily attach our personal value to our material success. It also helped me understand why shopping can feel so comforting, especially after a rejection or a loss. This simple concept can illuminate many of the underlying motivations we have for our financial behaviors, and I encourage you to think about how your possessions, especially those that most represent the parts of yourself you care about, are actually extensions of your identity. How do your personal items like your home, car, clothes, hobby gear, pictures, electronics, and your thousands of other things reflect who you are?

The possession–self link can be a powerful motivator for spending money, but I also believe it can be used to our advantage. For example, letting go of possessions that represent parts of your identity that you have outgrown can be an incredible feeling. In her book *The Life-Changing Magic of Tidying Up*, Marie Kondo speaks about how liberating it can be to let go of material things. Most of us have either experienced or heard someone recounting the intense pleasure of purging unneeded belongings during a move, a divorce, or a particularly deep cleaning. Still, while there is enormous pleasure to be found in letting go of material items, many people still struggle with overspending for emotional reasons.

Shopping for Fun or Sport For some of us, shopping is itself a strategy for meeting deeper needs. Some shop to combat boredom. Some like the hunt for a bargain. Some find it soothing to buy something new when we are feeling blue or rejected. For many people, shopping is a social activity. In her film, *Born to Shop*, Sarah Gibson reveals how stores are like playgrounds for our psyches where we discover novel objects that resonate with our inner desires. Shopping can be a form of play, an act of celebration, or a way to soothe a damaged ego, but we need to remember the cost we pay is permanent, while the emotional benefit is not.

Since our brains incorporate the things we own into our sense of self, everything we own or buy becomes a part of who we feel we are. This isn't character weakness or materialism; this is just the way our brains organize the world. Even people we feel close to get incorporated into our sense of self. The result is that our identities are a mix of our bodies, minds, personalities, relationships, and possessions. When we experience a loss or rejection, our sense of self is damaged or diminished temporarily. Experiencing a breakup, for example, can be a devastating loss to one's identity if that person was a large part of one's sense of self. Even things that seem small, like an insult or a passing look of judgment, can serve as threats to our identity. When our egos are depleted through fatigue, rejection, identity threat, or loss, our sense of self is diminished. Naturally, we will want to restore ourselves to the previous sense of fullness, and buying an object that represents who we *want* to be is a simple way to fill in the lost part of our identity.

I believe this is the psychological root of retail therapy. When one part of our identity feels threatened or damaged, we know that we can quickly fill in the gap by adding something new. Some studies have shown that when people feel judged or are afraid of being judged, they are more likely to buy on impulse, and it is especially true if the items they are presented with fit with their ideal sense of identity.

If retail therapy is a common strategy for you, remember this: The positive emotional effect is very short-lived, but the money you spend is gone forever. With some other areas of spending, I advocate finding strategies that are *less* expensive. With retail therapy, I think it's best to break the habit altogether. Going into a sales environment when you feel insecure or vulnerable is rarely a good idea. This is exactly the type of scenario where interventions are your best bet. Spend time with a friend, soak in a hot tub, write, play, and do whatever it takes to get back in touch with the fact that you are already whole without adding a new item to your list of possessions. You've heard that it's not a good idea to go grocery shopping when you're hungry. The same holds for other types of shopping. Do not shop when you feel small.

My personal weakness is clothes and home decor. I can, and have, done serious damage to my bank account because I love clothes and I love to redecorate fairly often. I love the feeling of a new outfit or a freshly decorated room that represents my best self (possession–self link? You betcha!), and I especially find myself compelled to shop for these things when I am feeling insecure or I have experienced rejection of some kind. These are my triggers. Clothes and decor are my familiar strategies. When I started to understand that in these moments, what I really want is to connect with my best self, to remember my strengths and feel hopeful about my future, I was able to find more effective ways to get back on track without spending. Going for a run, taking a hot bubble bath, painting my nails, playing guitar, dancing, journaling, meditation, yoga, sleep, and preparing a beautiful, healthy meal are all ways I have found to gently restore my sense of self after a loss or a disappointment. It's important to find alternatives to retail therapy *before* you're tempted to indulge.

What to Do about It

Retail therapy, or shopping to feel better, is a very common practice. Unfortunately, it can wreak havoc on your long-term financial goals, so how do you resist the urge to splurge? Science comes to the rescue here in the form of affirmations.

Affirmations Yes—affirmations, again. What's great about affirmations is that they work, and they are *easy.* Here's why they work in this context. When you experience a loss or a rejection, or even when you are simply tired or hungry, you are experiencing ego depletion. The idea here is that we have only a limited amount of self-control or willpower to draw on, and when our reserves are drained we have a harder time resisting temptation. Fatigue, mental strain, stress, and hunger can all work as drains on our self-control resources.[48] Research shows that stigma or the threat of rejection can also reduce self-control through ego depletion,[49] so stereotype threat can be a trigger for overspending if you use retail therapy. However our egos get worn down, the effect is the same: We have less self-control. So, when we are ego depleted, just trying harder to resist temptation will only work against us, making us more tired and more ego depleted. Instead, if we want to resist the temptation to shop when our egos are drained, the solution is not to be hard on ourselves, but to focus on replenishing our resources. This is where affirmations come in.

Researchers who study ego depletion have found that spending just a couple of minutes affirming core values can completely eliminate the negative effects of ego depletion.[50] These affirmations don't have to have anything to do with money. Apparently, simply reflecting on what is important to us can restore our sense of identity and replenish our reserves of self-control. With this in mind, I encourage you to try the following intervention next time you feel like a little retail therapy is in order.

▶ Write down two or three of your most important values. Using just a sentence or two, put each one on a separate note card.
▶ Carry these cards in your wallet.
▶ The next time you feel tempted to spend in order to feel better, take out the cards and read them to yourself.

Affirming your core values may help you avoid the financial harm of emotional shopping. You can write about your love of nature, your concern for equality, or your deep respect for honesty. What matters is that you write about something that is truly important to you. Thinking about your core beliefs can strengthen your self-control in the moments you need it most.

Rules for Safe Shopping When you *do* go shopping, it's good to have some ground rules rooted in the desire to avoid emotional spending.

The rules I outline here have been incredibly useful for me because of my particular needs and emotional triggers. I share them here because others have also found them very helpful in their own lives. These rules have not only saved me tens of thousands of dollars and immeasurable buyers' remorse, but they have turned shopping into an experience of empowerment and self-respect rather than an act of financial self-sabotage. Remember, I tend to splurge on clothes and home decor. You may need to tailor these rules to fit your particular shopping tendencies.

> **Rule #1: No matter how you feel, do *not* go shopping dressed in anything you do not feel fabulous in.** Stores and malls are painstakingly designed to dazzle and impress. If I walk into a store dressed in anything less than my best, I know I will be easy prey for my own insecurities. For this reason, I am intentional about shopping. If I am headed to any store where I might be tempted to shop emotionally, I dress up, put on makeup, and remind myself that confidence is not for sale. This is my equivalent to eating a snack before going to the grocery store.

> **Rule #2: Set a reasonable budget before you set out, and take it in cash.** I do not go shopping without first setting a limit that I know will not sabotage other needs. If that limit is $10, so be it.

> **Rule #3: Do not buy anything that you don't like as much or more than your current *favorite* thing.** Lots of things are nice. Many of them are great bargains. That's not a good enough reason to buy them. If my spending limit is very restrictive, that just makes it an exciting treasure hunt. This rule is not only important for my financial well-being, but I have noticed that it changes how I feel when I leave a store empty-handed. Before I started using these rules, I would often feel embarrassed to leave a store without buying something. Now, I feel empowered. By saying "no" to items that don't truly meet my needs, I am saying "yes" to financial security and self-actualization.

> **Rule #4: For every new item you buy, donate or discard an old one.** If I add a new favorite shirt to my closet, my least favorite thing goes to consignment. If I buy a new household item, I find

something I don't love and donate it. This rule benefits me in three ways:

1. Every new purchase upgrades my wardrobe or my home.
2. It keeps me from collecting clutter.
3. It reminds me that every purchase is a tradeoff.

As you work with your own needs and examine your own strategies, you may find some areas where you want to set some other rules for yourself. If you like to fix or build things, and find that you spend too much on parts and tools, maybe you could limit yourself to projects that only require one new tool. Each project will upgrade your toolkit, but you won't break the bank by getting into something too big all at once. Maybe you love to cook, but you find yourself spending hundreds on exotic ingredients that go to waste. You could limit yourself to one new recipe a week. Your needs, your strategies, your rules.

Time and Money: Why We Always Want It NOW

Emotions aren't the only reason why we can often be impulsive with our money. It can be incredibly hard to put tomorrow's needs ahead of the ones we feel today, especially because our minds are programmed to discount the future.

The Big Idea

Perhaps the *greatest* barrier to good financial behavior is our tendency to care more about today's desires than we do about our future needs. In general, people tend to prefer a smaller, immediate reward over a larger one that we have to wait for. Scientists call this phenomenon *discounting* because it refers to the way that we mentally shrink the value of things that are far off. Discounting the future is responsible for many types of behaviors that get in the way of our long-term goals, from procrastination to drug addiction, impulsive shopping, and failure to save money for the future.

Discounting is pervasive. We see evidence of it everywhere. We think we will go to the gym tomorrow, because the cost of working out feels smaller when we think of it happening tomorrow, and the couch feels really comfortable right now. We know we should save more, but retirement feels so far off, and going out to dinner would be really fun right now. Some of the time, the decisions we make are small and inconsequential, but a thousand little decisions to spend today rather than save for tomorrow add up to a huge problem when we suddenly need money for a health problem, a car repair, a baby, or when it comes time to retire.

Underlying Factors

Some people discount the future more than others, and the more we discount (read: the less patient we are), the more this can threaten our financial health. The good news is that researchers have found ways to reduce how much we discount the future. To understand how these work, though, it's important to know what causes discounting in the first place.

Impulsiveness On the one hand, there is a person's trait-level impulsiveness. This particular aspect of discounting has been a major focus of my research. Impulsiveness is a personality factor, and personality traits are pretty stable. A lot of research shows that personality factors are not likely to change with small interventions, but impulsiveness and discounting are strongly linked. Now, if impulsiveness makes a person discount the future heavily, and impulsiveness can't be changed, then we might as well conclude that being good with money is a genetic trait, and there's nothing that can be done about it. If you are impulsive, does that mean a death sentence for your finances? I wanted to know, and the results of my research offer some hope for people who are highly impulsive or impatient.

The truth is that changing your personality is pretty difficult, and maybe not even desirable. Why should you have to change who you are in order to be financially stable? If you are a highly impulsive person by nature, overcoming the effects of discounting will be a big challenge for you, but it is possible. What I found in my work is that there are other mental factors that *can* be changed through simple interventions and activities, and these other mental factors can not only directly help you be better with money, but they may even be able to reduce a bit of your impulsiveness in financial decisions.

If you are curious to know just how impulsive a psychologist would say you are, you can answer the questions in the Brief Self-Control Scale (BSCS), included in the self-assessments section. (Appendix A, How Impulsive Are You?) This quiz is used in many academic studies as a measure of trait-level impulsiveness, and your score can help you figure out if your financial issues are related to this personality trait. If they are, don't worry. While a low score on the BSCS means that you are at greater risk for high debt levels and impulsive spending, it also means that there is a specific set of activities that are likely to help you to be better with your money.

A person's impulsiveness is closely related to how they think about time because patient and impatient people actually experience time differently. Did you catch that? Patient and impatient people experience time differently! A time delay feels longer to impatient people than to patient people. When you think about how waiting feels to different people, it makes a little more sense why impatient people would discount the future more. The time you have to wait for something is part of the cost of that thing, so if time feels longer to impatient people, then the cost of waiting is actually higher to them than it is to patient people. If you are impulsive (impatient) then waiting is actually a more painful experience for you than your patient peers, and you will have a stronger preference for shorter time delays.

However, if you have ever tried to change your personality, you know how difficult this can be. Thankfully, you don't have to. Instead, there are a couple of simple mental tricks you can use to make the future seem closer, and these seem to promote more patient financial behaviors. These little mental "hacks" work by changing how far away the future *feels*, or what psychologists call *psychological distance*.

Psychological Distance Physical distance refers to how far away something is. Psychological distance is how far away something *feels*. Physical distances are objective; a mile is a mile no matter where it is on the globe, and a year is a year no matter when it happens in history. Psychological distances, on the other hand, are subjective; a year may feel short to one person and incredibly long to someone else.

Psychological distance is at the root of our discounting behavior. The further away something feels, the more we discount it, and we do this with more than time. There are at least four dimensions of psychological distance: time (now vs. later), space (here vs. there), relationships (me vs. them), and probability (guaranteed vs. impossible). When something is psychologically close, we put a higher value on it than something that is psychologically distant. Clearly, you will care more about what will *definitely* happen to *you* in the *here* and *now* than what *might* happen in the *future* to a *stranger* on the *other side of the world*. That's psychological distance at work.

The discounting effects of psychological distance explain many of people's preferences and reactions. Why did Americans react so strongly to the Boston Marathon bombing and barely notice the café bombing in Baghdad that happened days earlier? Because the Boston Marathon was in Boston (physically closer), and many of the victims were Americans (socially closer). As the mother of an elementary school student, I found the Sandy Hook shooting incredibly traumatic because it hit "close to home." The events were not physically close, but Sandy Hook was very much like my own community (social closeness), making the events feel very close to me psychologically. We all know the feeling of being "too close" to something or someone to have an objective point of view. We have laws that require doctors and judges to recuse themselves from professional service when they are "too close" to a situation or person to be objective. There is even an old adage, "He can't see the forest for the trees," that describes a person who is so caught up in the details of a problem that they cannot see the big picture. In truth, neither way of viewing a scenario is better than the other. They simply focus on different aspects of the thing you are thinking about. A high-level construal is like a bird's-eye view of a situation or thing, while a low-level one is a close-up view. All of these scenarios involve psychological distance.

Psychological distance primarily affects the way we handle our money by affecting our mental picture of the future and how we feel about our future self. We can change the psychological distance between today and the future by using something called construal level.

Construal level refers to how we mentally picture something. If we picture (construe) an event or a person in broad, abstract terms, that is a high-level construal. From high up, you don't see the tiny details, but you get the big picture. A high-level description of a person might be, "She is very nice and hard-working." Low-level construal focuses on the details, and is more concrete. A low-level description of the same person might be, "She is a 27-year-old Latino woman with two children and a bachelor's degree." We tend to think of things that are psychologically distant in high-level terms, and use low-level construal for things that are psychologically closer. For our purposes, let's just call construal level *mental imagery*, because that's actually what it is.

When we think about things that are far off, we tend to picture them using high-level imagery. From a distance, we see the forest. When something is closer on any of the dimensions of psychological distance (time, space, relationships, or likelihood), we focus on finer details. We see the trees. For example, think about traveling to spend the holidays with your favorite friends or family members. When that holiday is six months away, you will be thinking about it in abstract terms. You might think about making memories, relaxing, continuing traditions, or just enjoying time together. These are all high-level views of a holiday. As the day gets closer, you will start to think in more concrete, low-level terms. You will think about what clothes you need to pack, where you will park, what gifts you will give, and what your specific itinerary will be. We naturally adjust our thinking depending on psychological distance, and our brains are so used to this process that if you force yourself to think about the distant future in fine detail, you can trick your mind into shrinking the psychological distance so that it feels closer. Doing that will make that future feel more likely, and therefore more emotionally charged, and it can make the needs of your future self feel more immediately important.

While we can change our mental imagery depending on the situation, each of us has what is called a *chronic construal level,* which just means that we have a certain way that we tend to picture the world. Some of us are big-picture people, and others are more detail oriented. High-level people think about *why* something is done, and low-level people think about *how.* Again, each way of thinking has its own strengths, and they serve very different functions. We need visionaries, but we also need the people who can execute on that vision. A highly functioning team would likely have both types of people. Our chronic construal level affects the way we approach life and tackle problems. It affects what we are motivated by and how we plan, and, as it so happens, your chronic construal level can determine the way you should set your savings goals.

What to Do about It

One of the most fascinating pieces of research, in my opinion, that has come out in recent years with regards to saving behavior was published in the *Journal of Marketing Research* in 2011. The researchers had a large group of undergraduates think about something they planned to save for within a month's time. They asked half of them to set a specific dollar amount (low-level goal), and the other half to set a more general goal to save as much as they could (high-level goal). The researchers also had everyone take a test to find out what their chronic construal level was. This resulted in four groups (see Figure 3.1).

Then, the students came back a month later and reported on how much they had actually saved for their goal.

Can you guess which people saved the most? When I first read the study, I assumed that everyone who set a specific dollar amount would

Experiment Groups		Goal Type	
		Specific	General
Construal	High	1	2
Level	Low	3	4

Figure 3.1   Saving Study: Four Groups

save more than those who kept their goal vague and nonspecific. The actual results were far more interesting. As it turned out, the people who set a goal that was *in contrast to their normal way of thinking* were the ones who saved the most. High-level thinkers who set a specific dollar amount and low-level thinkers who kept their goal nonspecific saved far more on average than the people who kept their goal consistent with their chronic construal level (see Figure 3.2).[51]

Use Mental Imagery to Save More It would seem that there is not one particular way to view your goal that works best, but rather that introducing a *contrast* to your normal way of thinking is the key. These findings are exciting to me because they point to a very simple way we might be able to help ourselves save more. It is not hard to diagnose yourself as either a big-picture person or a details person. Most of us already have a sense of which type we are. If you want to take a more scientific approach, you can use the same test that Ülkümen and Cheema used for their research called the Behavior Identification Form (Appendix A).

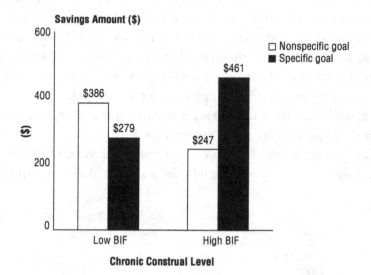

Figure 3.2   Who Saved the Most?
Source: G. Ülkümen and A. Cheema, "Framing Goals to Influence Personal Savings: The Role of Specificity and Construal Level," *Journal of Marketing Research* 48 (2011): 958–69.
Note: BIF = Behavior Identification Form

Once you know what your chronic construal level is, you can choose the savings strategy that is best for you. If you are a high-level thinker, you will want to set a specific dollar amount to save by a certain time. If you are a low-level thinker, keep your goal broad, and just focus on saving as much as you can in that time.

Get Chummy with Your Future Self Another mental trick that can help you save more money uses the social and time dimensions of psychological distance. Dr. Hal Hershfield, assistant professor of marketing at the Anderson School of Management at UCLA, has done some great work showing that the way we feel about our future self can have a big influence over how we handle our money.

Imagine yourself 10 years from now. How similar do you think your future self will be to the person you are today? How much do you like that person you are picturing? How clearly can you picture that future self? Psychological distance theory tells us that a very similar future self will feel closer (socially) to us than a future self who is very different. Construal level theory tells us that if we picture something in "vivid and realistic terms," it will feel psychologically close. If you like the future self you are imagining, that is also a sign of social closeness rather than distance. So, it makes sense that if you picture your future self as being *similar* and *likeable*, and you picture them *in fine detail*, you won't discount their needs as much as you would if you had only a vague image of some unlikable person who barely resembles who you are today.

> *Specifically, when the future self shares similarities with the present self, when it is viewed in vivid and realistic terms, and when it is seen in a positive light, people are more willing to make choices today that may benefit them at some point in the years to come.*
> —Hal Hershfield[52]

Dr. Hershfield and his colleagues showed that people who interacted with a detailed avatar of their future self made more patient financial choices as a result.[53] I believe that the detailed picture of this future self forced a low-level mental picture onto what people would normally think about in broad, abstract terms. The age-progressed image essentially shrank the psychological distance between their present and future selves.

I said before that we can overcome some of our impulsiveness by using the idea of psychological distance. Ultimately, by reducing the psychological distance between your present and future self, you can make the future *feel* more real and important, and more patient financial behaviors are a natural side effect of caring more about the future you.

If you don't believe me, you can try it for yourself. Dr. Hershfield's work has been incorporated into a free age-progression app developed by Merrill Edge and Bank of America,[54] but any age-progression application will do the trick. Take a look at this age-progressed version of you, and try to get comfortable with the fact that this is your future. Many psychologists recommend making peace with your inner child; I am a big advocate for getting cozy with your inner senior citizen. By really facing your future, thinking about it in fine detail, and creating a sense of closeness with the person you will be in 10 or 20 years' time, you will naturally make the needs of your future self feel more important, and hopefully you will start to make some positive financial decisions that will help you prepare for your future needs.

Get Clear about the Future In my own work, I wanted to know about the combined effects of impulsiveness and future self-continuity on financial decisions. Since impulsiveness makes us less patient and future self-continuity makes us more patient, which one wins in a fight? When it comes to our financial behaviors, is personality or mental imagery more important? To answer this, I surveyed hundreds of people and asked them about their financial habits using the Financial Management Behavior Scale (included in Appendix A for your reference)[55] and their impulsiveness (using the BSCS), and then I asked two questions about their mental concept of the future. For the first, "When you think about the future, how far ahead do you tend to think or plan?" answers could vary from "Less than a week" to "More than 10 years." The second question asked, "How clear and detailed is your mental picture of the future?" Answers were on a scale from "Extremely vague and without detail," to "Extremely clear and detailed." I also asked about their materialistic values and gave them the Big Five financial literacy questions.

When impulsiveness and future concept are both competing for control over our financial decisions, who wins the fight? The future concept wins, and in a very interesting way. Not only was the direct effect of a person's future concept on their financial management score larger than the direct effect of impulsiveness, but there was an added, indirect effect of the future concept on financial behaviors by way of reducing impulsivity. The results suggest that the further a person thinks into the future, and the clearer and more detailed their mental picture is, the more that will dampen the effects of impulsiveness on financial behaviors. This finding may be especially useful for people who score low on the self-control scale (BSCS). It would appear that having a clear and detailed picture of the future can effectively reduce the impact of impulsiveness on your finances.

What was unexpected, and very interesting to me, was that among people who did not use credit, the effect of impulsiveness on financial behaviors was no longer significant to the model (Figures 3.3 and 3.4). In other words, not using credit cards got rid of the impact of trait-level impulsiveness altogether. Among the people who didn't use credit cards, having a clear and detailed future concept still increased positive financial behaviors, but impulsiveness didn't affect financial behaviors at all.

Figures 3.3 and 3.4 are illustrations of how each mental factor relates to financial behavior. The connecting lines represent relationships between factors, with arrows indicating direction of effect. For example, Financial Literacy has a direct effect on Financial Behavior, but not the other way around. The numbers near the lines indicate how strong the relationships are (higher = stronger). A positive number means that the factor is positively related and a negative number shows an inverse relationship. You can see (Figure 3.3) that a person's future concept is negatively related to Impulsiveness, and positively related to Financial Behavior.

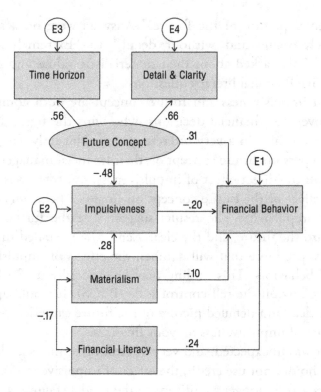

Figure 3.3   People Who Use Credit

So, if you are highly impulsive, and you can't trust yourself to rein in spending on your own, then you might want to consider eliminating credit cards from your life. There are other ways to build good credit, and if you know yourself well enough to conclude that access to spending is dangerous for you, then follow in the footsteps of my study participants, and make that impulsiveness moot by staying away from credit cards. On the other hand, if you are impulsive, but you think you can keep yourself in check, then you might see some good results simply by creating a very clear picture of your future in 10 years' time.

The bottom line here is that if you want to be better with money, but you are impulsive, instead of changing your personality, you can change the way you picture the future. You can age-progress your face,

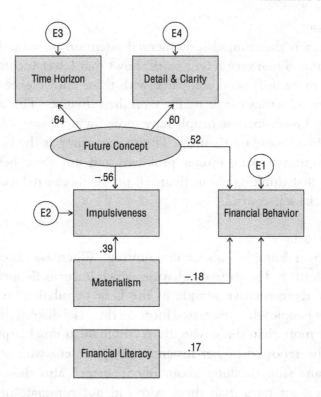

Figure 3.4   People Who Don't Use Credit

or you can simply visualize your future in vivid detail. However you do it, make sure you add detail and clarity to your mental imagery because that brings it close up in your mental view, decreasing the psychological distance. In doing so you may find that you are internally driven to save more in order to care for your future self.

If that doesn't work, cut up your cards.

Thinking in Circles

We saw before that thinking about money can produce a rational, achievement-oriented mind-set. That's when we think about money itself, and it acts as a boost for self-reliance and persistence. On the other hand, when we ruminate on money *problems,* instead of triggering an attitude that fosters achievement, we end up with lower self-control.

The Big Idea

Rumination is the compulsively focused attention on something that is distressing. Some very recent work shows that lower-income people ruminate more in general compared with those with higher incomes, but in particular they ruminate more on their finances. This isn't really surprising. Lower-income people have more financial stress. Of course they ruminate more on finances. The strange thing is the connection between ruminating on money problems and impulsive behavior. It turns out that thinking about financial problems can reduce patience and financial self-control.

Underlying Factor

By now, you know all about discounting. When we discount the future, it leads to less patient behavior, which hurts us financially. In a nationally representative sample of the U.S. population, researchers found that people who ruminated more on financial distress discounted the future more than those who didn't ruminate as much. Specifically, people who reported higher instances of agreement with statements like, "I can't stop thinking about my finances," also showed much higher discount rates than those who did not ruminate on money. Financial ruminators were also more likely to take on bad debt than those who did not ruminate.[56] This means that fixating on our financial problems can weaken our self-control, which leads to bad financial decisions.

When we're in trouble financially, it can easily consume our thoughts. We think that by going over the details in our mind we will be able to solve the problem, so we go in circles, ruminating on our financial stress and situation. The ironic—and important— finding from this research is that when we fixate on our financial problems, we actually make them worse. Rumination increases discounting, which makes us less likely to save and prepare for the future. The very thing we *think* will help us solve our financial problems (thinking about them over and over, trying to solve them) turns out to put us at higher risk for even more money issues down the line.

What to Do about It

But how can we reduce rumination behaviors? If you tend toward this kind of thinking, what can you do to break the habit? The researchers in this area found that distracting yourself when you notice rumination starting can help, at least temporarily. To be clear, this does not mean that you should ignore your financial difficulties and spend money as if you had plenty to burn. On the other hand, fixating on the problem doesn't help either.

If you are a ruminator, it may be best to train yourself to change your focus when you notice yourself going in circles or fixating on the stress. Remind yourself that ruminating will make it worse, and do something fun (and preferably free) to get your mind to move on to other things. When you are not fixated, you will be better able to recognize opportunities and solutions when they arise. A relaxed mind is a creative mind, and you will make better financial decisions when you do not exhaust yourself by stressing about your financial situation. Easier said than done, for sure. Still, with science on your side, you can remind yourself that rumination is a financial killer all by itself. Distract yourself, take a deep breath, and return to life with a little more peace of mind. You will find a way, and you will find it more easily when your mind is freed up to recognize it. At last, you have a really good reason for watching cat videos.

Finances and Emotions

Ruminating on finances is an extreme example of having a negative emotional experience with your money. Even if you do not ruminate, you may experience stress, sadness, fear, or anxiety (remember, more than half of us are losing sleep over money). You may also feel satisfaction, joy, or peace when you think about your money. What determines this? Is our emotional experience with money based solely on how much we earn? Can the way we think about time affect our emotional experience with money?

The Big Idea

The way we picture the future, and the ideas we have about the amount of control we have in our lives, both affect the emotional experiences we have with our money. This means we may be able to improve our financial satisfaction even if we don't increase our paycheck.

Underlying Factors

In a small study conducted at HelloWallet in 2015, I looked at how a person's concept of the future affected their emotional experiences with money. We know that thinking further into the future has a positive impact on financial behaviors, but what about on our emotions? In this study, I found that regardless of how much money a person was earning, their future concept had a powerful effect on the emotional experiences they had with respect to their finances.

The Future and Emotions Figure 3.5 shows how people's future concept related to their emotional experiences with money over a six-month period, broken down by income group. The left cluster shows that on average, everyone whose mental picture of the future was vague and without detail had mostly negative emotional experiences with money. This was true no matter how much money they were making.

On the other hand, the right cluster shows that when people had a highly detailed picture of the future, they had mostly positive experiences

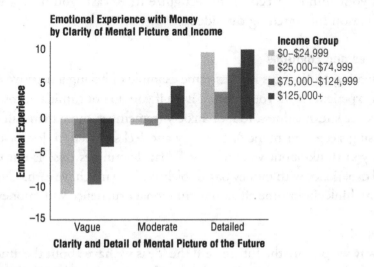

Figure 3.5   Time and Emotions

with their finances. They reported more joy, satisfaction, and peace as well as less fear, anger, and sadness regardless of whether they were making less than $25,000 or more than $125,000. This was a small study, and certainly needs follow-up research, but it appears that not only does having a clear picture of your future make you better with money, it also makes you enjoy it more.

Control and Emotions Do you believe that what happens to you is mostly the result of chance, Fate, or the like? Or do you believe that you create your own destiny? Of the people I have surveyed, those who believe they create their own destiny have much more positive emotions when dealing with their money than people who believe that the events in their lives are determined by chance, Fate, or the like.

Figure 3.6 shows people's emotional experiences with money, broken down by their views on control over their own destiny and their income group. People in the left cluster think they are masters of their own fate, and those on the right feel that they mostly don't control what happens to them. Across all income ranges, people who believe they are the masters of their own fate experienced mostly positive emotions concerning their money. This is striking because the people making less than $25,000 per year were having positive emotional experiences, as were the people making $125,000 or more. However, almost without exception, people who had a neutral view or felt that their lives were not determined by their own actions had mostly negative experiences with their money. They reported feeling more fear, stress, anger, and helplessness. The only exception was the group making more than $125,000; they still had mostly positive experiences, but as their sense of control over life dropped, their experiences moved close to being negative.

These results, though they are from a small group (only about 115 people), suggest that the ways that we think about time and the center of control in our lives can have a very strong effect over the emotions we experience with money. It would appear that having a more peaceful and positive relationship with money is not just about earning more or behaving differently, but also how we think. These

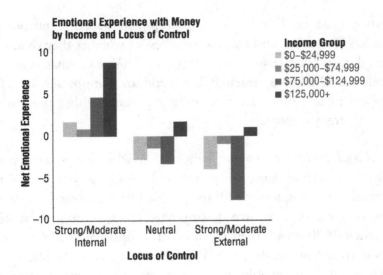

Figure 3.6   Control and Emotions

results show that even if you never become rich, you can still be happy with your financial life. If we look only at the group of people earning less than $25,000, we can see that the people who had an internal sense of destiny were experiencing peace, joy, and satisfaction in their finances, while those who believed they do not control their lives felt fear, anger, and sadness. Looked at in another way, it would seem from these results that in order to compensate for the negative emotional effects of believing that your life is determined by external forces, you would need to earn more than $125,000 per year or more.

Whether you believe that Fate determines your life or that you determine your own destiny is a deep and personal belief, and it is not easily changed. Still, if you are looking for a way to find more peace and satisfaction in your financial life, but you don't anticipate making six figures anytime soon, this may be something worth looking into. By cultivating an internal sense of control in your financial life, and developing a clear mental picture of your future, you might find financial peace without even needing a raise.

What to Do about It

I have already mentioned a couple of techniques for adding detail and clarity to your mental picture (age progression, visualization), and the entire second half of this book is devoted to teaching a new way of thinking about money management that encourages a deeper sense of personal control over your financial life. The LOADED budgeting method was designed to help improve your emotional experiences with money while you make sound financial decisions that meet your present *and future* needs.

Financial Knowledge

The last mental factor I want to mention before moving on to more practical strategies for managing money is knowledge. Obviously, the amount that you know about how the financial world works, and how your money can shrink or grow over time, will make a big difference in the kinds of financial decisions you make.

The Big Idea

We need to know more about how money works. As I mentioned previously, the state of financial literacy in America (and, to be fair, around the world) is abysmal. Efforts to educate people about financial concepts have had mixed results, and so a lot of people have given up on financial education as a means of improving people's financial lives. It's important to note that when I say there have been mixed results, I do not mean that people with a lot of financial knowledge still tend to make poor financial decisions. On the contrary, the link between financial literacy and good money management is very clear. Many, many studies show that people with more financial knowledge tend to have higher incomes and more savings, and make better decisions about debt and credit.[57] The problem is not that knowledge isn't useful. More knowledge does lead to better decisions. The problem is that many of our efforts to teach people are simply not working. We don't retain the information long enough for it to be of real use, and sometimes the information is just too complex to be meaningful.

What to Do about It

Unfortunately, much of the financial world is intentionally complex, and becoming more complicated every day. Even people with advanced degrees in finance can often find the legal and technical aspects of some financial products difficult to understand, so what is the average person to do? Some people hire a financial advisor. This can often be a very good decision, but it is not appropriate for everyone. Most financial advisors are interested in clients who have at least $250,000 in liquid investable assets. In other words, your house doesn't count. If you have $250,000 or more that is available to be invested right now, then a financial advisor may be a very good resource for you. Even so, you will want to vet them carefully. The financial "services" industry is largely made up of salespeople who sell financial products that seem like services, and I daresay that the majority of people don't know the difference. There are some great advice columns and websites to help you understand the critical difference between a financial salesperson and a financial advisor, but the bottom line is that if you plan to use a financial advisor, give careful attention to how they are paid. If they get paid when you buy particular investments, or when you move your money around, then their interests and yours may not be well aligned. Some advisors are fee-only. Others are paid a commission when you buy certain investments. Others get paid when you move your money from one investment to another. Ask any potential advisor about fees, commissions, or financial incentives they receive other than the check you write them for their services.

If you are not yet in a position to hire a financial advisor, there is still hope. Research into which kinds of financial education work best have revealed two themes that seem to show some promise. These are just-in-time education[58] and rules of thumb.[59]

Just-In-Time Education Just-in-time education is exactly what it sounds like. You learn about the topics you need to know right at the time you need to know them. If you are not currently thinking about buying a home, learning about the different types of mortgage options available to you may not be very useful, and you might not retain the details of that information. On the other hand, if you are house-shopping now, or thinking about how much of a home you can afford, this is the perfect time to read up on mortgages. We are much more likely to pay attention and to retain the information when it is immediately useful to our lives. This is great news because it means that you do not need to go out and master every part of the financial world all at once. Instead, you can seek out information on the specific decisions you face when they arise.

The downside to just-in-time financial education is that the people who have the knowledge to give you do not know when you will need it. Thousands of free or inexpensive resources have been developed to teach people about any and every financial decision they may face. However, the people who created these resources don't know when someone is going to be buying a house, opening an IRA, saving for college, thinking about a payday loan, or trying to save on groceries. With just-in-time financial education, the burden is on the person who needs the information to go out and seek it. This can be a huge drawback because it leaves the door open for scammers or predatory financial "services" people to jump in and give you self-serving advice before you know better than to take it. The best way to protect yourself from bad financial advice is to seek out many sources, or to look for advice from sources that operate independently from banks or financial institutions. Government websites such as MyMoney.gov, the Jump$tart financial education clearinghouse, and many other resources are available to you for free. Use them as a starting point when you have a specific financial decision to make.

Rules of Thumb The second effective financial education strategy is to use rules of thumb. Especially among people who are not highly financially literate to begin with (most of us), learning rules of thumb has been shown to be a better strategy than learning more complex concepts. One study in the Dominican Republic compared two groups of business owners who took accounting classes. The first group was given a typical course that used "the standard approach to small business training, teaching the fundamentals of financial accounting." This course had *no measurable effect* on out-comes. The second group was taught simple rules of thumb, and this group experienced "significant improvements in the way businesses managed their finances."[60]

Rules of thumb are great tools because they are easy to remember and they can apply in many different circumstances. I believe that they work well because they utilize our natural tendency to simplify the world. I have already mentioned how rules of thumb (what behavioral economists call heuristics) can work against us. The good news here is that once we clear out the mental clutter and challenge the core beliefs that our unchecked heuristics and biases have created, we can replace them with more *useful* rules of thumb that are based on sound economic and psychological principles. You can spend years trying to learn and memorize all of the details about loans, for example. You can agonize over questions like, "Should I take out loans to go to school?" A rule of thumb would be really handy in this case. If you think about it simply using the rule of thumb, "Don't borrow more than you expect to earn in your first year after college," this enormous life decision becomes more manageable. Rather than getting bogged down in the technical aspects of the financial system, rules of thumb help us make financial behaviors much more simple. The rest of this book is dedicated to presenting a money management approach that blends psychology and economics to create a simple, empowering new way to look at the money in your life and a deeply fulfilling relationship with your money. Along the way, I present several rules of thumb to help guide you through some of the choices you will face as you begin to advance in your financial life.

Making Change
We have covered a lot of ground already, touching on many of the forces that underlie our financial habits. We've discussed the money messages that surround us from birth, and the personal money narratives that they create in our own lives, for good or ill. We've considered the negative impacts of poverty on both physical and mental health, and the positive and negative effects that thinking about money can have on

behavior. We've also examined the social orientations that money promotes in our socioeconomic groups. We've seen how our material possessions interact with our identities, and how discounting the future can play tricks on our mind and alter our priorities. And we've seen how our perspective on where the center of control in our lives resides can affect how we feel about our finances, regardless of our income. Along the way, we have looked at ways to intervene in our own minds to counter or lessen the negative effects of each of these mental factors on our own behaviors. As a quick reference guide and overview of all of these topics, use the chart in Figure 3.7. Whether you are looking to change your financial behaviors, the emotional experiences you have with money, or both, the chart that follows will guide you to the particular exercises that can help you retrain your mind for better outcomes.

All of the self-assessments listed in Figure 3.7 are included in the appendices, which also include several simple activities to help you explore and challenge core beliefs, increase your connection to the future and your future self, train compassion, and affirm core values. These simple activities can help you to clear away some of the mental clutter and will hopefully retrain the financial behaviors that are affected by your view of time and your more problematic core beliefs about money.

A few of the mental factors that contribute to our financial experiences are a bit trickier to change, and involve learning a new way of thinking about how money moves in our daily lives. Some core beliefs need to be changed through experience and a new way of seeing our financial realities. Whether or not you believe you control your fate is not an easily changed belief, and new rules of thumb can't be pulled from thin air. If you believe that your financial challenges are all centered on easily changed beliefs, and how you view the future, then you may find the interventions at the back of this book are all that you need in order to transform your financial life. If, on the other hand, you would like to learn a new way to manage your money that is based on sound economic rules of thumb, and is intended to help you feel a stronger sense of control and flexibility in your financial life, while also achieving a higher level of satisfaction with the money that you have, then the LOADED budgeting method was designed for you.

Behavior/Experience	Self-Assessment	Appendix A (Self-Assessments)	Interventions and Exercises	Appendix B (Interventions and Exercises)
Financial Behaviors	Financial Management & Behavior Scale	✔	Determine the mental factor(s) at work, and use the interventions below	
Financial Emotions	HelloWallet Pilot Study	✔		

Mental Factor	Self-Assessment		Interventions and Exercises	
Core Beliefs	Personal Narrative Exercise	✔	Change the narrative	✔
			Find a counterexample	✔
	Narrative Consolidation	✔	Work with the LOADED budgeting method	✔
Impulsiveness	Brief Self-Control Scale	✔	Age progression	✔
Discounting	Brief Self-Control Scale	✔	Future Visualization/Mental Contrasting	✔
Future Self-Continuity	FSC scale	✔	Age progression	
Future Concept	Horizon & clarity	✔	Future Visualization/Mental Contrasting	
Construal Level	Behavior Identification Form	✔		
Locus of Control	LOC measure	✔	Work with the LOADED budgeting method	
MoneyThink			Loving-kindness meditation	✔
			Write about equality	✔
			Get Awed	✔
			Commune with nature	✔
Ego Depletion & Emotional Spending			Affirm core values	✔
			Work with the LOADED budgeting method	
Knowledge	Big Five Financial Literacy Questions	✔	Just-in-time education— Seek it out!	✔
			Rules of thumb (LOADED budget method)	
LOADED Budget Method			Cash Flow Worksheet	✔
			Resources Worksheet	✔
			Expenses & Needs Worksheet	✔
			Personal Economy Worksheet	✔

Figure 3.7 Assessments, Activities, and Worksheets

The rest of this book moves away from the abstract world of the mind, and outlines a simple money management technique that blends psychology with economics to foster a healthy and empowered relationship with your money. In the language of psychological distance, we will move away from the abstract reasons for why we behave the way we do, and delve into the concrete details of how we interact with our money on a day-to-day basis. This money management strategy is intended to bring your sense of financial control inward, as well as give you insight into emotional spending habits, and concrete strategies to change them. Along the way, I offer simple rules of thumb that can help you make sound financial decisions in many types of situations.

Thus far, we have touched on many of the reasons that money is a loaded topic. Now, we will move on to discuss how to use your money in such a way as to feel like you *are* loaded. The LOADED budgeting method ultimately blends the abstract and the concrete together to form a holistic strategy for your money that integrates the "how" of budgeting with the "why" of personal satisfaction. The result is a money management plan that is uniquely tailored to you. Built on a foundation of simple economic principles, it will help you make positive and strong financial choices, yet since it incorporates psychology, you will find that the plans you make using this method do not lead to feelings of limitation or self-denial as so many budgets do. If you have tried budgeting plans before and felt deprived or suffocated by them, if you have attempted to change your spending behavior in the past and failed, or if you simply want to organize your money in a way that feels deeply satisfying instead of limiting, the LOADED budget will help. I have personally used this money management strategy to transform my own financial life, and I will never go back to the traditional money management methods. It is not a scheme to make you rich, though you may use it to do so. More importantly, the LOADED budget teaches a way of organizing and understanding your financial life that can help you reach a place of deep personal satisfaction by creatively channeling your resources to meet all of your personal needs, regardless of the numbers you are working with.

Notes

1. American Psychological Association, *Stress in America: Paying with Our Health* (Washington, DC: American Psychological Association, February 4, 2015), www.apa.org/news/press/releases/stress/2014/stress-report.pdf.

2. American Psychological Association, "American Psychological Association Survey Shows Money Stress Weighing on Americans' Health Nationwide," news release, February 4, 2015, www.apa.org/news/press/releases/2015/02/money-stress.aspx.

3. Sienna Kossman, "Poll: Americans Sleeping Better as Economy Recovers," CreditCards.com, June 24, 2015, www.creditcards.com/credit-card-news/financial-worries-losing-sleep.php.

4. American Psychological Association, *Stress in America.*

5. Christine Bahls, "Achieving Equity in Health," *Health Affairs,* October 6, 2011, www.healthaffairs.org/healthpolicybriefs/brief.php?brief_id=53.

6. American Psychological Association, *Stress in America.*

7. Bahls, "Achieving Equity in Health."

8. Margot Sanger-Katz, "Income Inequality: It's Also Bad for Your Health," *The Upshot* (blog), *New York Times,* March 30, 2015, www.nytimes.com/2015/03/31/upshot/income-inequality-its-also-bad-for-your-health.html. Low-income people pay a larger portion of their available resources, or worse, go into debt and pay interest on top of the cost of care.

9. Bahls, "Achieving Equity in Health."

10. Ibid.

11. For an excellent review of the research on poverty traps, see Samuel Bowles, Stephen N. Durlauf, and Karla Hoff, eds., *Poverty Traps* (Princeton, NJ: Princeton University Press, 2011).

12. Sandro Galea et al., "Urban Neighborhood Poverty and the Incidence of Depression in a Population-Based Cohort Study," *Annals of Epidemiology* 7, no. 3 (2007): 171–179; Deborah Belle and Joanne Doucet, "Poverty, Inequality, and Discrimination as Sources of Depression among U.S. Women," *Psychology of Women Quarterly* 27 (2003): 101–113.

13. Richard Zwolinski, "An Overview of Depression and Money Issues," *Psych Central,* July 9, 2010, http://psychcentral.com/lib/an-overview-of-depression-and-money-issues/.

14. Janice Wood, "Money Arguments Are Top Predictor of Divorce," *Psych Central,* 2013, http://psychcentral.com/news/2013/07/13/money-arguments-are-top-predictor-of-divorce/57147.html.

15. Institute for Divorce Financial Analysts, "Survey: Certified Divorce Financial Analyst® (CDFA®) Professionals Reveal the Leading Causes of Divorce," accessed December 31, 2015, www.institutedfa.com/Leading-Causes-Divorce/.

16. B. Claussen, S. Davey, and D. Thelle, "Impact of Childhood and Adulthood Socioeconomic Position on Cause Specific Mortality: The Oslo Mortality Study," *The Journal of Epidemiology & Community Health* 57, no. 1 (2003): 40–45.

17. Y. H. Khang, "Relationship between Childhood Socio-economic Position and Mortality Risk in Adult Males of the Korea Labour and Income Panel Study (KLIPS)," *Public Health* 120, no. 8 (2006): 724–731.

18. J. M. Guralnik, "Childhood Socioeconomic Status Predicts Physical Functioning a Half Century Later," *Journal of Gerontology: Medical Sciences* 61A, no. 7 (2006): 694–701.

19. Claussen, Davey, and Thelle, "Impact of Childhood."

20. Eric Jensen, *Teaching with Poverty in Mind: What Being Poor Does to Kids' Brains, and What Schools Can Do about It* (Alexandria, VA: ASCD, 2009).

21. Jean-Claude Croizet, "Extending the Concept of Stereotype Threat to Social Class: The Intellectual Underperformance of Students from Low Socioeconomic Backgrounds," *Personality and Social Psychology Bulletin* 24, no. 6 (1998): 588–594; Bettina Spencer and Emanuele Castano, "Social Class Is Dead. Long Live Social Class! Stereotype Threat among Low Socioeconomic Status Individuals," *Social Justice Research* 20, no. 4 (2007): 418–432; Chetan Sinha and Arvind Kumar Mishra, "Revisiting Social Class: Exploring Stereotype Threat Effect on Intellectual Performance of School

Students," *Journal of Educational Sciences and Psychology* 65, no. 1 (2013): 133–146.

22. Steven J. Spencer, Claude M. Steele, Diane M. Quinn, "Stereotype Threat and Women's Math Performance," *Journal of Experimental Social Psychology* 35 (1999): 4–28.

23. "What Is Stereotype Threat?" accessed December 31, 2015, www .reducingstereotypethreat.org/definition.html.

24. Becca Levy, "Improving Memory in Old Age through Implicit Self-Stereotyping," *Journal of Personality and Social Psychology* 71, no. 6 (1996): 1092–1107.

25. Nai Chi Jonathan Yeung and Courtney von Hippel, "Stereotype Threat Increases the Likelihood That Female Drivers in a Simulator Run over Jaywalkers," *Accident Analysis & Prevention* 40, no. 2 (2008): 667–674.

26. Jennifer K. Bosson, Ethan L. Haymovitz, and Elizabeth C. Pinel, "When Saying and Doing Diverge: The Effects of Stereotype Threat on Self-Reported versus Non-verbal Anxiety," *Journal of Experimental Social Psychology* 40, no. 2 (2004): 247–255.

27. Yeung and von Hippel, "Stereotype Threat."

28. Ryan M. Pickering, "Getting to the Heart of Social and Educational Disadvantage: Exploring the Impact of Social Interactions across the Class Divide," 2014, Order no. AAI3581309, available from PsychINFO (1676370818; 2015–99080–203).

29. N. John-Henderson et al., "Wealth, Health, and the Moderating Role of Implicit Social Class Bias," *Annals of Behavioral Medicine* 45, no. 2 (2013): 173–179.

30. Kathryn L. Boucher, Robert J. Rydell, and Mary C. Murphy, "Forecasting the Experience of Stereotype Threat for Others," *Journal of Experimental Social Psychology* 58 (2015): 56–62.

31. Sabine C. Koch, Stephanie M. Müller, and Monika Sieverding, "Women and Computers. Effects of Stereotype Threat on Attribution of Failure," *Computers & Education* 51, no. 4 (2008): 1795–1803.

32. Karen Wright, "When Money Talks," *Psychology Today*, May 1, 2009, www.psychologytoday.com/articles/200904/when-money-talks.

33. Brandon J. Schmeichel and Kathleen Vohs, "Self-Affirmation and Self-Control: Affirming Core Values Counteracts Ego Depletion," *Journal of Personality and Social Psychology* 96, no. 4 (2009): 770–782.

34. N. M. Stephens, H. R. Markus, and S.S.M. Townsend, "Choice as an Act of Meaning: The Case of Social Class," *Journal of Personality and Social Psychology* 93, no. 5 (2007): 814–830.

35. For a fun and lively overview of Piff's work, see his TED Talk: www .ted.com/talks/paul_piff_does_money_make_you_mean?language=en.

36. K. D. Vohs, N. L. Mead, and M. R. Goode, "The Psychological Consequences of Money," *Science* 314 (2006): 1154–1156.

37. Ibid.

38. Agata Gasiorowska, "Money Cues Increase Agency and Decrease Prosociality among Children: Early Signs of Market Mode Behaviors," *Psychological Science* (forthcoming).

39. Ibid.

40. Paul K. Piff, "Wealth and the Inflated Self: Class, Entitlement, and Narcissism," *Personality and Social Psychology Bulletin* 40, no. 1 (2014): 34–43.

41. Jia Wei Zhang et al., "An Occasion for Unselfing: Beautiful Nature Leads to Prosociality," *Journal of Environmental Psychology* 37 (2014): 61–72.

42. Paul K. Piff et al., "Awe, the Small Self, and Prosocial Behavior," *Journal of Personality and Social Psychology* 108, no. 6 (2015): 883–899.

43. Paul K. Piff et al., "Having Less, Giving More: The Influence of Social Class on Prosocial Behavior," *Journal of Personality and Social Psychology* 99, no. 5 (2010): 771–778.

44. Thomas G. Plante, *The Psychology of Compassion and Cruelty: Understanding the Emotional, Spiritual, and Religious Influences* (Santa Barbara, CA: ABC-CLIO, 2015).

45. James Grubman, *Strangers in Paradise: How Families Adapt to Wealth across Generations* (Turner Falls, MA: FamilyWealth Consulting, 2013).

46. R. Belk, "Possessions and the Extended Self," *Journal of Consumer Research* 15, no. 2 (1988): 139–168.

47. Ibid.

48. Martin S. Hagger et al., "Ego Depletion and the Strength Model of Self-Control: A Meta-Analysis," *Psychological Bulletin* 136, no. 4 (2010): 495–525.

49. M. Inzlicht, L. McKay, and J. Aronson, "Stigma as Ego Depletion: How Being the Target of Prejudice Affects Self-Control," *Psychological Science* 17, no. 3 (2006): 262–269.

50. Schmeichel and Vohs, "Self-Affirmation and Self-Control."

51. G. Ülkümen and A. Cheema, "Framing Goals to Influence Personal Savings: The Role of Specificity and Construal Level," *Journal of Marketing Research* 48 (2011): 958–969.

52. Hal Hershfield, "Future Self-Continuity: How Conceptions of the Future Self Transform Intertemporal Choice," *Annals of the New York Academy of Sciences* 1235, no. 1 (2010): 30–43.

53. Hal E. Hershfield et al., "Increasing Saving Behavior through Age-Progressed Renderings of the Future Self," *Journal of Marketing Research* 48 (2011): S23–S27.

54. You can find the Merrill Edge app at https://itunes.apple.com/us/app/face-retirement-from-merrill/id815224857?mt=8.

55. J. Dew and J. J. Xiao, "The Financial Management Behavior Scale: Development and Validation," *Journal of Financial Counseling and Planning* 22, no. 1 (2011): 43–60.

56. Gita Johar, Rachel Meng, and Keith Wilcox, "Thinking about Financial Deprivation: Rumination and Decision Making among the Poor," in *Advances in Consumer Research*, vol. 43, eds. Kristin Diehl and Carolyn Yoon (Duluth, MN: Association for Consumer Research, 2015), 208–211.

57. J. S. Hastings, B. C. Madrian, and W. L. Skimmyhorn, "Financial Literacy, Financial Education and Economic Outcomes," *Annual Review of Economics* 5 (2013): 347–373.

58. D. Fernandes, J. Lynch Jr., and R. Netemeyer, "Financial Literacy, Financial Education and Downstream Financial Behaviors," *Management Science* 60, no. 8 (2014): 1861–1883.

59. A. Drexler, G. Fischer, and A. Schoar, "Keeping It Simple: Financial Literacy and Rules of Thumb," *American Economic Journal: Applied Economics* 6, no. 2 (2014): 1–31.

60. Ibid.

4

The LOADED Budget
Creating a Human-Centered Money Management Plan

Up to this point, we've been talking about how we think and feel about money in a very personal sense. We've discussed the complex relationship many of us have with money, the stereotypes that accompany both poverty and wealth, and some of the specific mental and cognitive factors that can influence our financial behaviors.

Having a healthy relationship with money requires that we first remove the negative and damaging beliefs and perspectives that underlie our self-sabotaging habits. By now, you have likely singled out and begun to challenge some of the specific thoughts, feelings, and beliefs that have held you back from having peace in your financial life. I encourage you to continue working with these insights in the coming weeks and months. You will find that while old habits die hard, they do, with perseverance, die. This is also true for habits of thinking.

The next step is to replace our old patterns of thinking with new ones. Here, we will make a shift from the abstract to the practical. This section will teach you a new way to look at how money moves in your life, from how it is generated to how it is used. Beginning with the traditional approach to budgeting, I will show you why I believe this method is problematic from a psychological perspective, and offer you a new, more empowering way to think about the money in your life. I've also provided worksheets so you can start to put these concepts into use with your own finances.

The goal of this section is nothing less than a paradigm shift. The LOADED budget method puts *you* at the center of your financial life, and builds a budget around you and your priorities. I strongly encourage you to use the worksheets and get very specific about your financial circumstances. However, many of the concepts in this section can be distilled to simple rules of thumb that you can use in many situations.

What's Wrong with Your Budget?

Most of us were taught to budget using what I call the Cash Flow model. This very simple, two-column budget will be familiar to most of you (Figure 4.1).

In the Cash Flow model, you add up your income and subtract your expenses. Anything left over goes to savings. Some people practice

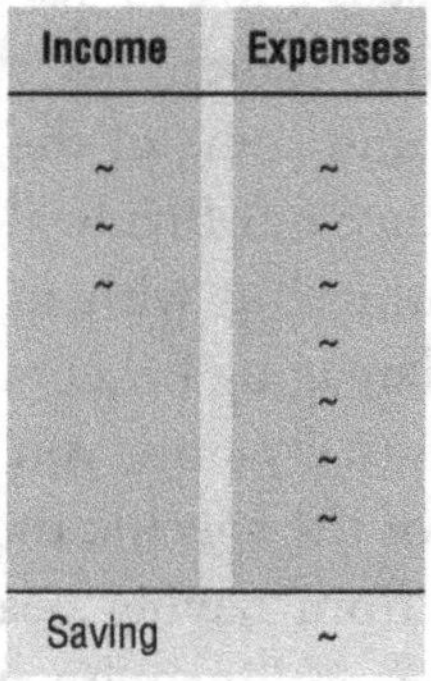

Figure 4.1   Cash Flow

a "pay yourself first" method where they list their savings as their first expense. Either way, this model of money management is pretty basic: two columns, all numbers, end of story.

Income and Expenses: How the Cash Flow Model Works against You

While the Cash Flow method of organizing income and expenses is certainly practical, it has some problems when viewed through the lens of psychology. In general, this method is all about flow, which makes intuitive sense, but where is the money flowing *from?* Where is it flowing *to?*

In the Cash Flow model of budgeting, money is like a river (Figure 4.2). It flows in as income, and it flows back out as expenses. According to this

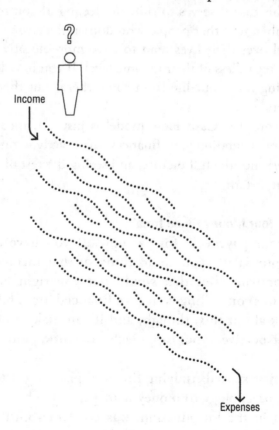

Income

Expenses

Figure 4.2   Cash Flow

model, money flows in and out of your life, and your job is to direct the flow—and hopefully divert some of it into a little pool for yourself called savings.

This is a very *dis*empowering way of thinking about your money.

When I ask people in workshops where their money comes from, I generally get answers like "my job." Occasionally, I've heard "the Treasury" or "my parents," but one thing all of these answers have in common is that they view money as coming into one's life from an outside source.

If we picture money coming in from some faraway place, we put psychological distance between our income and ourselves. You already know that psychological distance has many effects on financial behavior, but in this case it serves to shift the feeling of control away from you. Remember, too, that people who don't feel a strong sense of personal control over their lives tend to have more negative experiences with money, regardless of their income level. If you have learned to see money coming into your life from somewhere "out there," then this applies to you.

What's more, the Cash Flow model is just . . . incomplete. This method of understanding your finances isn't exactly wrong, but it's the *end of the story*, not the full picture, and seeing the rest of the picture is incredibly important.

Where Does Your Money Come from?

Let's take your paycheck, for example. If you have an employer who pays your salary, you could think of that income as coming from the company. But that would put you right back into the mind-set of not controlling your own financial life. There is another way to think about this, though, and it can make a big difference in your perspective, your approach to work, and your future income.

When I first started studying financial planning, I took a course that applied psychology to money management. The professor, who I introduced in the Introduction, was Dr. James Grubman: a psychologist and financial expert who had spent years counseling people through the challenges of managing great wealth. In a lecture that would drastically change the course of my life, he explained to the class, "When people find themselves suddenly wealthy, either through business success or some other windfall, some of them will keep their wealth and even pass it on to the next generation, but others quickly find themselves back where they started." Then he asked the big question: "What is the *psychological* difference between the people who maintain that wealth and those who do not?" We ventured a few feeble guesses, and then he laid out the simplest and most surprising explanation I have ever heard. What separates those who maintain great wealth from those who lose it? Over more than 20 years of experience, Dr. Grubman had learned what financial planning books don't teach: "What I have seen is that those who make the transition from thinking about money in terms of *income* to thinking about money in terms of *assets* are the ones who successfully adapt to wealth, and maintain it."

This simple observation stuck with me. Over the years, I have come to understand the psychological factors that may be responsible for what Dr. Grubman had seen in his clients. To me, the best part about Dr. Grubman's insight is that the simple shift in thinking that he deemed responsible for *maintaining* wealth is also quite a powerful tool when it comes to *building* financial security, regardless of where you start out.

There is a very good reason why thinking about money in terms of assets is helpful to maintaining and growing wealth, and it is the exact same reason why the Cash Flow method of budgeting is inadequate. A Cash Flow budget is a simple record of inflows and outflows, but it fails to give any attention to the source of income or the purpose of expenses. What Dr. Grubman noticed when he saw that some people made a shift in their thinking from income to assets is that these people understood *where their money was coming from*. They saw a bigger picture than those who only thought about income. What is that bigger picture, and how does it relate to assets? If income is a river, then an asset is the spring. Focus on maintaining a healthy spring, and you will always have a steady flow.

Income and Assets

Every stream of income in the Cash Flow model of a budget can be traced back to an *asset* that has financial value. In the case of your paycheck, the asset generating that income is the *labor* that you devote to your employer. Your time, energy, and intelligence all combine to create something of value to your employer: labor (Figure 4.3). If you add specialized knowledge or practical experience, the value of your asset increases, generating a larger potential income stream.

Does your salary come from your employer? Not at all! Your employer is simply renting your time and skills. Your salary is the result of your internal resources being turned into a valuable asset that *you lease to your employer* in the form of labor. Your skills are the asset. Your salary comes from you.

Why is this distinction so important? First, remember that in my research, I found that people who had a sense of controlling their own destiny generally had more positive experiences with their money. A simple shift of focus away from your employer and to your own role in generating your income could have a positive emotional benefit even if it doesn't change your situation. Second, by focusing on the source of income rather than the flow, you will be better equipped to make many types of beneficial financial decisions down the line.

Asset	Income	Expenses
Skilled Labor →	~	~
	~	~
	~	~
		~
		~
		~
		~
Saving	~

Figure 4.3 Assets Generate Income

Rule of Thumb: Focus on the Spring, Not the Stream

If you focus on nurturing and protecting the resources and assets that generate your income streams, you are more likely to preserve a steady income in the long run.

Think for a moment about the prospect of losing your job. In a scenario where you are laid off, your income from labor stops flowing, but what has happened to your asset? Have you actually lost the source of your income? No, you've simply lost a buyer. All of your assets are likely still intact. You still have your time, energy, and intelligence. You still have your skills and your experience. In fact, you have probably built up a stronger portfolio of experience and skills since you first started your job, so your asset may be even more valuable than it was when you were initially hired. The network of contacts and relationships you built during your time there are also valuable resources you can use to help move forward in your career. With this knowledge in mind you can set about finding a new buyer for your skills with the confidence that your asset is as valuable as it ever was.

This way of thinking helps us think about protecting and nurturing the assets we have, rather than just directing the flow of income they produce. Skills lose value if they are not honed and upgraded over time, so to protect the value of your asset, it is wise to keep learning and acquiring new skills and knowledge. If you are not paying attention to the fundamental value of the asset generating your paycheck, you might not see the importance of continuing education, networking, and skill building after you settle into a job that you love.

Three Income Sources Most of us are familiar with labor as a source of income, even if we've never thought of our labor as an asset that we sell. From childhood we are asked, "What to you want to *be* when you grow up?" What this question is often really getting at is, "How will you earn a living?" Few of us were taught early on to think about the other two income sources besides labor: land and capital. If you've ever taken an introductory economics course, you've heard about land, labor, and capital as the three factors of production. Every income stream on your cash-flow sheet can be traced back to one of these three things.

Labor creates income when you trade your time, energy, and talent for money.

Land has the potential to generate income in all sorts of ways. You can farm it, mine it, rent it, sell it, harvest and sell its trees, or build on it and rent the property out to others. Sometimes, even if you do nothing with it, land increases in value over time as other properties around it are developed. The increase in value is a form of income because you can sell the asset for more than you paid.

Capital is a little harder to define, but you can think of it as anything (other than land and labor) that has inherent financial value. There are a few types of capital: physical, financial, and social. Physical capital could be anything from the clothes in your closet to the roto-tiller in your shed. Physical capital represents potential income because it can be sold or rented in exchange for money or other goods.

Financial capital is simply money. Whether it is in the form of savings, investments, cash, bonds, or gold, money itself can create more money by earning interest when you lend it to individuals, banks, or governments.

Social capital can be hard to put into actual dollars, but still can make a difference to your finances. Do you have a good reputation? You're more likely to get a solid job reference. Have you helped others when they hit hard times? They'll likely help you out when you need it most. Social capital has great potential to generate income and reduce expenses. If you can borrow for free rather than buy, your income will go further. If you have a strong professional network, you will hear about the best jobs and promotions when they become available. Quite often, people trade in social capital through babysitting co-ops and nanny shares, or bartering services with friends and neighbors. Swapping expertise and building collaborations is not only useful and saves money; it often builds even deeper connections, too.

One young company in Boston is working with banks and local businesses to help people who give time to their community to earn points for discounts on household items and local services. While most of us can't cash in our social capital in quite such a literal way, the old adage, "It's not what you know, it's who you know," can very often be true. Personal networks can make a big difference in finding good work and trustworthy services. Whether it saves you money through carpooling or gets your foot in the door for an important interview, your social network can have a big effect on your finances.

How Do I Know if Something Is an Asset? Since assets are such an important part of generating income, it's important to have a clear definition of just what an asset is. If you look up the word *asset* in a dictionary, you will get a very broad definition such as, "a useful or valuable thing, person, or quality." That's true, but pretty vague, and it doesn't make any reference to actual income potential. If you ask an accountant or a financial manager, you will get a more technical definition like, "property owned by a person or company, regarded as having value and available to meet debts, commitments, or legacies." Again, this is accurate, but it's very technical and limited to physical property, so it doesn't really suit our purposes.

What I want to offer you is a rule of thumb that helps to simplify a very complex financial world. For this reason, I believe the best and most useful way to think about assets is this: *An asset earns more money than it costs.* I'm sure there is an accountant somewhere who is cringing at this definition because it glosses over some fine technical points. So be it.

Rule of Thumb

It's not an asset unless it earns more than it costs.

This definition is also helpful in understanding the importance of building up assets other than labor. If you ever want to stop working, you have to have other forms of income to cover your expenses. That means you have to have enough land and/or capital to replace the income from your labor. Some people call this retirement. Some call it being independently wealthy. It's all the same. When your income from assets other than labor is enough to cover all of your expenses, you can safely stop working. Some people are born with enough assets to avoid labor all their lives if they want to. Some reach this point in early adulthood. Most of us strive to stop working by the time we are in our mid- or late 60s. Some will always need to work. Regardless of which path you are on at the moment, the Cash Flow budget misses this point altogether. If we focus only on the flow and not the source, we miss the bigger picture. Using only a Cash Flow budget is like traveling a long journey with only a small piece of the map. You will get somewhere, but will you get where you *want* to go?

Seeing this bigger picture is an important step in taking charge of your financial life, but we're not done yet. The real magic happens when we broaden our view just a little bit more. We know that assets produce income, and we know that there are three general types of income source: land, labor, and capital. Some people are fortunate enough to start life with assets but many of us are not. If we don't start with assets, then how do we get them?

Assets and Resources

Assets come from resources. If you have a beautiful piece of wood, tools, and woodworking skills, you're loaded with resources. Carve the wood into a handmade chair and you've created an asset. An asset is just a collection of resources put together in such a way that they create something that's valuable to others. It's true, we don't all start with assets, but we *all* have resources. We all have at least some time, energy, and intelligence to start with. Put those together, and you have labor. Add some education or training, and you have *skilled labor*. The heart—the very core—of making money is learning to combine your resources to create something of value to others. The beauty of this fact is that while some of us have more to work with than others, we all have at least some resources available to us.[1]

What Is a Resource?

A resource, in this context, is *anything that you have available to you for your use.* Your imagination, your sense of humor, your friends, your smile, the public library's Internet connection, the local community center, and the sunshine are all resources you can draw from.

Some resources are public and available to all of us, like libraries, schools, roads, museums, archives, parks, clinics, or community workshops. These resources are often free or available at very little cost. Other resources are quite personal and unique to each of us as individuals. Your particular personal genius, your imagination, your unique history and experience are all resources you can draw from to make your contribution to the world singular and valuable.

You're Already Loaded: Creative Resource Management

Quite often when we think of budgeting, we think of cutting expenses. We don't always think about what we could do to produce more income. When you start to understand that assets are just resources put to creative use, you will begin to see that your financial situation is not fixed. There is room for creativity and flexibility. When you take stock of all of your resources, you will realize that many of them may offer great opportunities for new streams of income.

Do you have extra room in your home? Taking on a roommate could bring in hundreds or more every month. Do you have items in your basement or attic that you keep meaning to donate? A few photos and posts on eBay or Craigslist might mean $50 or so a month in extra income. Do you have a skill or talent that you can teach to others? Teaching just one lesson a month could bring in enough to pay for your online video subscription. Your unused clothes could earn money from consignment, and cut your costs the next time you go shopping.

When we start to think about our resources like this, instead of feeling stuck in a tight place with our money, we begin to find some breathing room. Instead of a chore or a heavy weight, making money becomes a creative challenge. How can you use the resources you already have to generate a larger stream of income? With some imagination and creativity, your resources, however limited, can be turned into something valuable. Consider Cassandra's situation.

Cassandra's Story Cassandra was going through a divorce and adjusting to life as a single mother. As a student, she made very little. She was renting the house that her family had lived in for several years, but the expenses were more than she could handle on a third of her former income. Student loans helped, but they were not enough to meet all of the needs of her family, and she earned too much to qualify for government assistance. She was certain that once she graduated she could provide a good life for her family, but less certain that she could afford to reach the finish line. Many nights she lost sleep thinking through possible scenarios. Could she pick up a weekend job? Her research contract didn't allow that, and besides, most of that income would be gone after paying for the additional childcare. Moving into student housing would cut her expenses a bit, but they didn't accept pets, and her family had already been through enough loss without having to part with their beloved companions. Moving would cost money, too, and it could take a year before she would see any real savings. She seriously considered leaving school to work full time, but repaying her student loans without a higher degree would be just as unworkable. Cassandra needed a safe place for her family, but she felt burdened by a house that had once felt too small. It was too big to afford alone. That was the answer—the house was too big!

Cassandra cleared out the room that had once been her husband's home office, and had since become a playroom. She gave it a fresh coat of paint and new curtains, and put an ad online for a roommate. Within a month, she had found the perfect fit: a nursing student who loved kids and wanted to live in a family environment. By sharing her home, Cassandra's expenses dropped enough to make the house affordable. This strategy met more than her need for shelter. She found connection and support from a new friend, peace of mind from having a nurse in the house, and a powerful sense of autonomy and accomplishment from finding a way to reach her educational goals without putting her family through more strain and loss.

To start creatively thinking about resources and assets, try the following exercises. These should get your creative wheels turning, and hopefully spark some ideas about how to be creative with your own resources.

Exercises

Trace your income to your resources.

The first, and most obvious, application of this concept is to take a look at how you are currently turning your resources into assets, and how much income they are generating now. To do this, start with the Income column of your Cash Flow budget, and work backward from each stream of income to its source, as shown in Figure 4.4.

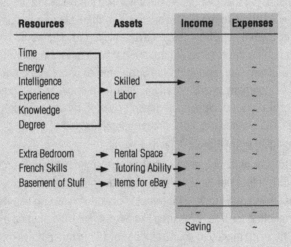

Figure 4.4   How Income Maps to Resources

Now ask yourself, are you using these resources to their full potential? Could you be generating more with them? Do you have any other resources you could list?

(Continued)

(*Continued*)

Resources List

If you have more resources in your life in addition to those you are already using to generate assets. Taking stock of them can help you get to the next level of income potential.

Use the blank Resources Worksheet in Appendix B to write down as many things you can think of to which you have access. What do you have? Who do you know? What do you know about? What are you good at? Do you have a skill you could teach in your community through an adult education class run by your town? What types of free classes or activities does your town offer where you could build new skills or network for a better job? You're loaded with resources. Take stock.

If you are having trouble thinking about your internal resources, you can try asking a few friends what they think your strengths are. Sometimes it helps to have an outside perspective to see the value we create in the world around us. Another way to brainstorm your resources is to think about what people ask you to do for them most often. If you have a pickup truck, I would bet that people ask you to help them move or haul things. You could consider putting your truck in a car share and renting it out by the hour to people who don't want to pay full rental company prices or only need it for an hour or so. Remember, too, that every effort to produce income doesn't need to be large. Simply taking your gently used clothes to a consignment shop instead of giving them away can bring in some extra money once in a while.

In addition to your personal resources, there are some public resources that may apply to you. The Internet provides some interesting and easy sources of part-time income; if you don't have an Internet connection, you can use the local library's connection for free. Websites like Mechanical Turk can be a great way to earn a little extra money in your free time by filling out surveys or categorizing pictures for researchers and companies that need the help. If you have specialized skills, you can find freelance opportunities on Fiverr, Upwork, or other sites that attract people who need specialized work done in small batches.

I encourage you to visit your town's website, go to your local university's cooperative extension website, and take a look at your local chamber of commerce or city government's web pages. Try a search for local mentoring clinics, free career advice, community workshops, training, and so forth. In my experience, I have seen many groups that put a lot of work and expertise into offering great resources to the community, but that are not always excellent at marketing those workshops or getting the word out. You might have to go digging, but chances are there are some great opportunities around you that you can use to learn, train, grow, collaborate, or just get ideas about how to make the most of what you have.

Resource Cards

Write each item you listed on your Resources worksheet on a separate index card. Then, mix them up and draw three at random. Using only those three resources, brainstorm how you could create an asset or reduce your expenses. The strategy doesn't have to be very realistic, and it doesn't have to be something you would truly consider doing. This is just to get the wheels turning and spark your imagination.

Once you're warmed up, start to think about more practical uses for your resources. Can you use your car and your free time to drive for a ride-share? Can you leverage your professional network and your skills to find a higher-paying job? Can you use the extra bedroom in your house, your loving family, and your choppy French language skills to host a foreign exchange student (host families earn a stipend)?

Before we move on, I want to make one last point about taking stock of personal resources. Up to now I have focused on the moneymaking potential of personal resources, but there is another important reason why you should take stock of your strengths, talents, and interests even if they don't have income potential. In the next section, we will discuss expenses and needs, and how to reduce expenses by creating new strategies to meet our needs. With this in mind, it's incredibly valuable to list as many resources as you can, not just those that are easily turned into cash. If you are someone who is good at bringing people together and creating community, for example, write that down. You may not be able to see how your resources are immediately useful, but don't worry about that now. The purpose of your Resources List is to take stock of everything you have, everything you are, and everything you can do. If, when you look at your Resources List, you do not feel *loaded*, then keep working at it. This exercise is simple, but that doesn't mean it's easy. Many of us are not accustomed to this kind of thinking, and it can take awhile to break through. Even if you cannot think of a single resource that could earn you extra money, make sure you put down your personal strengths, your physical capital (things you own), your financial capital, your social network, and your extra time.

Where Does Your Money Go?

Now, let's take a look at the other side of the Cash Flow sheet. In the same way that you can trace every income stream back to the resources that produce it, every expense can be traced back to a need. I'll discuss needs in much more depth a bit further on, but to balance out the concept of assets, I first want to talk about liabilities. Many items in the expenses column of a Cash Flow budget are generated by liabilities.

Expenses and Liabilities

Simply put, a liability is the opposite of an asset. Assets generate income by increasing in value or by earning more than they cost. Liabilities drain income by losing value over time, or by costing more money than they generate.

Again, we're not using the technical dictionary definition here, but this is a simple and practical way of understanding whether something is beneficial to your financial life, or a drain on your resources.

Rule of Thumb

A liability is something that costs more than it earns.

By this definition, many things in our everyday lives qualify as liabilities. Our children, pets, friends, social lives, and hobbies are all liabilities by this interpretation. Liabilities are not inherently bad or useless. They are simply things in our lives that cost more money than they produce. There are countless examples of things that are worth having even though they will never earn you a dime. The point here is simply to know which category something falls into. If it earns you more than it costs, it's an asset. Owning it will benefit your financial situation. If it costs more than it earns, it's a liability (Figure 4.5). Buying or maintaining it will require that you part with some income. Many of our expenses can be traced back to liabilities.

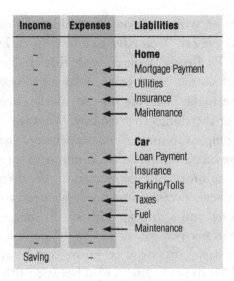

Figure 4.5   Liabilities Create Expenses

Should you try to eliminate all of your liabilities? No. For example, think about your social life. Other than the professional networking opportunities that might be mixed in with your relationships, the time you spend with friends and family can often cost money, but it is valuable in other ways. Your social life fulfills deep human needs, and to cut that out of your life because it isn't financially helpful to you would be irrational. The usefulness of this definition is not in labeling everything that costs more than it earns as something bad or to be avoided. Thinking about your financial life in terms of assets and liabilities is useful because it can help make major *financial* decisions easier, and it can shed light on which expenses are worthwhile and which you might want to rethink.

Expenses and Needs

Getting a Cash Flow budget to balance seems simple enough: When there isn't enough income, just cut back on some expenses. After all, the most fundamental part of money management is to spend less than you earn. Why, then, is this simple principle so incredibly hard for so many of us? I believe it's not that simple because *we're* not that simple.

This is a point on which I deviate from a lot of financial educators. We often hear people say, "You have to know the difference between a *want* and a *need*." I firmly disagree with this advice. After studying several theories of human motivation, I have become convinced that every decision we make is an attempt to meet a need. We *know* we don't need a lot of the things that we buy. We want them because we believe they will help us to meet some deeper need inside us. Even the frivolous items we buy on impulse are attempts to serve a fundamental need such as fun, comfort, ease, or relaxation. We do not need to learn the difference between a want and a need. We need to learn the difference between a *need* and a *strategy*. This small change of wording creates a big change in perspective.

When people say, "You need to know the difference between a *want* and a *need*," it draws a distinction between things that are necessary for survival and things that are not. This logic claims that if it isn't necessary for survival, then you don't need it, and if you don't need it, then you shouldn't buy it. That's a pretty strong money message when you think about it. There are some very austere values at play in that message. Maybe you agree with those values and maybe you don't, but let's examine the basic logic for a moment. Is it true that only things necessary for physical survival should be qualified as needs? Let's look at a famous model of human behavior that you may already be familiar with: Abraham Maslow's hierarchy of needs.

Defining Needs
Any introductory psychology student will recognize Maslow's Hierarchy of needs (Figure4.6.).

In the original version, these five sets of needs (Basic, Safety, Love & Belonging, Esteem, and Self-Actualization) are organized as a hierarchy. The theory loosely teaches that the bottom, basic needs must be met first before a person concerns themselves with higher needs. In Maslow's words,

It is quite true that man lives by bread alone—when there is no bread. But what happens to man's desires when there is plenty of bread and when his belly is chronically filled? At once other (and "higher") needs emerge and these, rather than physiological hungers, dominate the organism. And when these in turn are satisfied, again new (and still "higher") needs emerge and so on. This is what we mean by saying that the basic human needs are organized into a hierarchy of relative prepotency.

—Maslow, 1943, p. 375

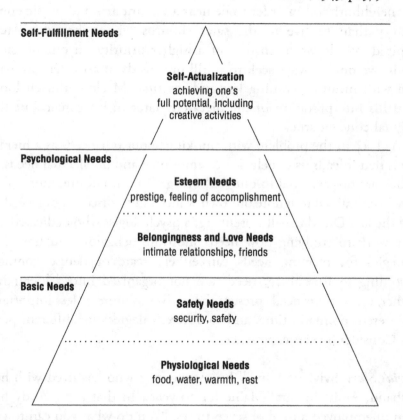

Figure 4.6   Maslow's Hierarchy of Needs

Over time, Maslow's theory has evolved, and others have built upon it, so that today there are at least seven categories of needs, including cognitive needs like the need for meaning, and aesthetic needs such as the need for beauty.

As good as this theory is, it is not perfect. It is not hard to think of examples of people who flip the hierarchy on its head. Some would rather go hungry than sacrifice their need for purpose or meaning. Many people of faith fast regularly, and one doesn't have to look far to find examples of people putting their needs for belonging and esteem above their need for safety (texting while driving is one example). Others might prefer to live in a relatively dangerous city neighborhood in order to be near a vibrant arts and music community than to live in the safer suburbs where they don't feel inspired. While we often do put a higher priority on our physical needs, we don't always seek to fulfill our needs in a ladder-like pattern with meaning coming last and sex first. Maslow himself loosened his interpretation of the hierarchy later in his career, but the original concept stuck.

As I see it, the problem with thinking about our needs as a hierarchy is that it leads us to belittle our emotional and intellectual needs as if they are not essential to our well-being. "In our culture, most of us have been trained to ignore our own wants and to discount our needs," said the late Dr. Marshall Rosenberg, a psychologist who dedicated his life's work to studying how needs motivate behavior, and how our strategies for meeting needs can either create or defuse conflict. According to Rosenberg, needs are not organized into a hierarchy. Rather, our various needs present themselves as more or less important at different points in time, and to different degrees for different people. Consider Sylvia's experience.

Sylvia's Story Sylvia is a small business owner who has lived with her husband, Andy, in rural Maine for 30 years. In that time, Andy has been unemployed a total of seven times. "You do what you can to get ahead," explains Sylvia. "You start to pay down the debt from the last unemployment, and then you're hit with another one, and then the car needs new tires . . . by the time you hit midlife you realize that all those dreams of being president and changing the world are just unrealistic. You have to find joy in the present because you're not going to be rich and famous and live the easy life. This is life."

Sylvia is incredibly resourceful, and has created a gorgeous home on a shoestring budget. For many years, she has frequented yard sales and junkyards, scouring them for the treasures that someone else discarded. She gardens and raises plants indoors to help in the long, colorless winters. While many praise her resourcefulness, for a long time she felt like her craving for a cozy home was something on the level of a mental illness. The desire was incredibly strong, yet she knew it wasn't a *need*. She thought that it must have been due to the particular tumult in her life that she felt so compelled, but she was sure she was the only one with this strangely powerful drive.

When Sylvia recognized that human needs are not based on a hierarchy, she saw for the first time that one of her deepest needs is for beauty. For her, having a beautiful, cozy home gives her a feeling of being safe in the middle of life's chaos. Sylvia reminds me of another lover of beauty, Coco Chanel. "People think that luxury is the opposite of poverty," Chanel once said, "but it is not. Luxury is the opposite of vulgarity." We can live in luxury with very little money if we are creative. A clean, cozy, beautiful space can be created from very little if you are resourceful. "If you're going to be poor, at least live someplace stunning," Sylvia says. I wholeheartedly agree.

Sylvia says that once she understood that having beauty in her life was a *real* need even though her physical survival doesn't depend on it, it changed her life. "It broke my brain open," she told me. "Now, when I go to a yard sale or the dump to find little treasures for my home, I don't feel crazy anymore. I feel proud." Sylvia has made beauty on a budget one of her highest priorities. Her income may never become steadier, but she lives surrounded by beauty, and that helps her make it through the harder days. She has reason to feel proud. She is not waiting for her financial situation to become more stable before living luxuriously, but she isn't breaking the bank to do it, either. "People want to get married in my living room," says Sylvia, "And I've done all this with no money!"

Sylvia's need for beauty is more important to her than many other things. Her resourcefulness allows her to meet her need without draining her bank account. This is the skill we need to master: not to discredit our needs by calling them wants and thereby denounce them as unimportant, but rather to validate and honor them by meeting them with strategies that don't sabotage our other needs, such as those for security and peace of mind. Anything short of this will leave you unfulfilled in some way, and a budget that leads to feeling deprived is not one you are likely to keep.

Why is it so important to recognize that all of our needs are important? Because ignoring a need does not make it go away. In fact, when we deprive ourselves of our deep needs, we often find that the need gets larger and our desires more pronounced. How many times have you tried to cut back on a certain expense only to find yourself splurging later? This comes from the fact that what we have called wants are actually needs. The core message of Rosenberg's work was that every action a person takes is intended (consciously or unconsciously) to meet a basic need, and that our needs are universal. Any one of our needs might feel more important than another in a given situation, depending on the person and the circumstance. On one day, you may feel a powerful need for intimacy. The next, you may desperately seek solitude. This theory fits more accurately with what I have personally experienced, and what I have observed in others. Beyond this, Rosenberg believed that conflict emerges when the *strategy* we employ to meet a need conflicts with another need. Finding peace in our financial life comes from creating better strategies, not from depriving ourselves of what we need.

What we are aiming for is a financial plan where *all* of our needs are met, but if needs are not hierarchical, then why bother with Maslow at all? Because, by looking at Maslow's hierarchy, we can see that some kinds of needs are better suited to financial strategies than others (Figure 4.7).

The needs that are at the bottom of Maslow's hierarchy—the basic survival needs—are corporeal, having to do with our physical bodies. As physical needs, they are usually met with physical items like food, shelter, and clothing. Due to their tangible nature, these physical needs often *require* financial strategies to be met. With the exception of homesteaders and farmers who hunt or grow their own food, most of us buy our food. Yet even homesteaders and farmers need to purchase

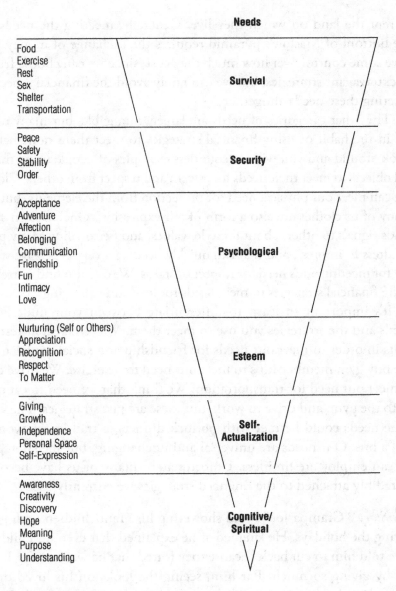

Needs

Food Exercise Rest Sex Shelter Transportation	**Survival**
Peace Safety Stability Order	**Security**
Acceptance Adventure Affection Belonging Communication Friendship Fun Intimacy Love	**Psychological**
Nurturing (Self or Others) Appreciation Recognition Respect To Matter	**Esteem**
Giving Growth Independence Personal Space Self-Expression	**Self-Actualization**
Awareness Creativity Discovery Hope Meaning Purpose Understanding	**Cognitive/Spiritual**

Figure 4.7   Needs and Money

or rent the land on which they live. Generally, meeting the needs on the bottom of Maslow's pyramid requires the exchange of money. We have some control over how much they cost, since we can choose frugal or extravagant strategies, but we can rarely avoid the financial aspect of meeting these needs altogether.

The other categories of needs are largely intangible, but many of us are in the habit of using financial strategies to meet them nonetheless. Look around and you will see countless examples of people using material objects to meet their needs for esteem and respect from others. Clothing can meet our physical need for protection from the elements, but for many of us clothes are also a form of self-expression. One's chosen style sends signals to others about lifestyle, values, and personality. Many people dress to impress, and that can quickly become a very expensive strategy for meeting one's need for respect or status. We can also find ourselves using financial strategies to meet needs for love and belonging.

It's important to learn to differentiate between your underlying needs and the strategies you use to meet them. We often eat at restaurants in order to meet our needs for friendship and social connection. We buy gym memberships to meet our need for exercise. We drive cars to meet our need for transportation. We think that we need to eat out, go to the gym, and drive to work, but these are just strategies. The very same needs could be met with potluck dinners, a trail in the woods, and a bus. Our needs are universal and unchanging, but the strategies we can employ are limitless. Unfortunately, many of us have become incredibly attached to the financial strategies we currently use.

Joe's Story "Grampa Joe" loved showering his grandchildren with gifts during the holidays. He laughed as he explained that even his children have told him to cut back because they feared that he was hurting himself by giving so much. For him, seeing the looks on his loved one's faces when they receive his gifts met very primal needs for love, belonging, and nurturing. He used these gifts to create a legacy for himself. He loved being viewed as a generous man, and seeing the excitement on his grandkids' faces when he came to visit. We can all understand Joe's needs. Still, his strategy for creating that sense of love and warm feeling was in direct conflict with other needs. If Joe were able to afford all of these gifts without sabotaging his financial security, this strategy would have been fine. However, behind the joyful, generous façade of "Grampa Joe" was a deep and growing debt. The problem with meeting emotional needs with financial strategies is that we can quickly exhaust our resources.

Joe was easily able to understand that his gift-giving habit was a strategy to meet his deeper need for connection to his children and grandchildren. He could also see how there might be other ways to meet these needs: by spending less money on gifts and more time on the phone or in person, for example. Joe's face dropped when he talked about these options, though. After some time, it became clear that Joe believed nothing else would replace the look of joy he saw when a grandchild opened a gift. Maybe he feared they would not value his visits as much if he cut back on gift giving. Maybe he doubted that his presence could be as valuable to his family as his generosity. Sadly, Joe was not convinced that he could meet the same emotional needs with a different strategy. What Joe is failing to see is that if he doesn't find a new strategy, he will end up dependent on his children for financial help. Instead of giving gifts to his grandchildren, he will be relying on gifts from his own children to survive.

Joe is not alone. Many of us are so accustomed to our current strategies that we find it very hard to see other options. Creative resource management is a simple idea, but that doesn't mean it's easy. It is, however, a crucial skill to learn if you want to achieve financial freedom. Some of our needs are well served by financial strategies, and others are not. Unless we have access to nearly unlimited resources, meeting emotional needs with financial strategies can be very, very risky.

Change the Strategy, Meet the Need

Erasing an item from your expenses column might make the numbers balance, but the need can't be erased so easily. In reality, a need can never be erased. You can cut your texting plan, but your need for connection isn't going to go away. You can cancel your cable subscription, but your need for relaxation won't be canceled. A budget has to feel better than what you are already doing, or else you won't keep it.

Very often, when people are trying to make ends meet, their first strategy is to start cutting expenses. While this is a great instinct, and we often *do* want to cut back on our spending, the problem with this approach is that if you do not take the time to ask yourself what need that expense was meeting, you will find that your new budget is very uncomfortable. Just like a dieter who restricts himself too much only to find himself eating an entire pizza in a late-night frenzy, we can do more harm to our finances than good by ignoring our needs when we cut our expenses.

For example, how many times have we all heard how much we could save by skipping your mid-afternoon trip to the coffee shop? "You could save $1,500 a year!" the experts say. So, you think, "Wow. That would pay for my health insurance premium. Great! I'm in!" and you start to make your coffee in the break room. And it works . . . for a couple of days. Then, as you are sitting under the fluorescent lights, listening to the air conditioning unit hum and staring at your equally bored colleagues, you realize that you want the smell of ground coffee beans and the sound of holiday jazz. You want to listen to the chatter of people in line and feel the cool air on your face as you walk back to the office.

If you have ever tried and failed to cut your expenses by skipping the coffee shop, it's probably because your need was not for coffee in the first place. By making coffee yourself, you eliminated the expense, but you didn't meet the real need. Maybe you're seeking human connection after hours of staring at a computer. Maybe you need a bit of relaxation, beauty, fun, or simply a change of pace to break up the monotony of the day. It could be that you have a need to connect with nature and the fresh air is what you're after. If you like to go with colleagues, you might be meeting a social need. Whatever it is, if you cut out an expense without devising a new strategy for meeting the need, you will find yourself unsatisfied (Figure 4.8).

Once you know the needs you've been meeting with a certain expense, you can start to create a new strategy to meet those needs

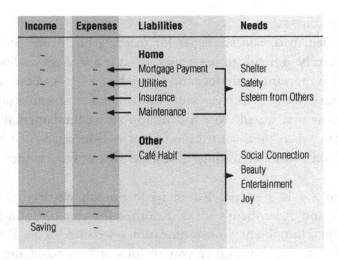

Figure 4.8 Expenses Come From Needs

without spending as much money. Sticking with the coffee example, if your daily coffee trip is meeting your need for social connection, you can invite a coworker to join you for break room coffee or a walk. If it's the sights and sounds of the city you enjoy, take your office mug for a walk around the block and soak it all in. If it's the smells and comfort of the café itself, try ordering the least expensive item on the menu. After all, now you know that you're there for the ambiance, not the caffeine.

Making and keeping a budget feels very restrictive to a lot of people. Even the word *budget* can conjure feelings of being limited and reined in. It does not have to be this way. We feel restricted when we fear that some of our needs won't be met. If we are mindful in our planning, we can create a life where all of our needs, physical, emotional, and intellectual, are met without draining all of our financial resources. That type of a plan does not feel restrictive, but deeply satisfying. The key to making this kind of plan is to remember that cash flow is just a part of the story. The real task we all have is to figure out how we can use our personal resources to meet all of our needs. When you become adept at this type of planning, you will find that many of your nonphysical needs are better served by nonfinancial strategies. This frees up your money to do what it is best at: meeting your physical needs.

Needs Are Universal

We get used to certain strategies for meeting our needs, and sometimes it can be difficult to tease apart what is a strategy and what is a need. It's important to understand that when we talk about needs in this context, we are talking about fundamental and universal needs. That means that we all share a common set of fundamental human needs that, when met, contribute to our well-being. When they are not met, they produce feelings of unease, discomfort, sadness, anger, or fear.

Figure 4.9 is a partial list of basic human needs that merges Maslow's and Rosenberg's ideas. Another list can be found at the Center for Nonviolent Communication's website.[2] This list is not exhaustive, but it should give you an idea of how basic and fundamental these things are.

Things Humans Need to Feel Satisfied (A Partial List)

Survival	Food	Sex
	Exercise	Shelter
	Rest	Transportation
Security	Peace	
	Safety	
	Stability	
Emotional	Acceptance	Fun
	Adventure	Intimacy
	Affection	Love
	Appreciation	Nurturing (self or others)
	Belonging	Recognition
	Communication	Respect
	Friendship	To Matter
Self-actualization	Challenge	Independence
	Giving	Personal space
	Growth	Self-expression
Cognitive/spiritual	Awareness	Hope
	Creativity	Meaning
	Discovery	Purpose

Figure 4.9   The Things Humans Need in Order to Feel Fulfilled

A quick scan of this list should make it perfectly clear how well suited some needs are to financial strategies, and how ill suited others are. Every single one of the needs listed *could* be met with any number of financial strategies, but it is not hard to see how a person could quickly outspend their income if they tried to meet all of their needs with money.

I cannot reiterate enough that every single item on the list is a *need*, not a want. In order to feel fully alive and satisfied, we need all of these things at one time or another. When we cut expenses that meet our needs, we are effectively saying that our needs don't matter, but they absolutely do! Every need is important, even though some are *more* important than others to each of us as individuals. Some people do not care much about having the respect or esteem of others, but for others those needs are paramount. To disregard your needs in order to meet your budget is a strategy that will leave you very unhappy.

Learning to distinguish between a strategy and a need is important for your financial health, and it can also be an incredible tool for resolving conflict over money in your relationships. Rosenberg's work was originally developed as a peacemaking communication tool. We know that money is one of the most common reasons for marital strife and divorce. This way of thinking has the power to heal your financial conflicts if you learn to think about needs and strategies, and to talk openly about them with your partner. The most important thing to remember when using this concept is that needs are universal, but strategies are not. In Rosenberg's words,

> Every moment each human being is doing the best we know at that moment to meet our needs. We never do anything that is not in the service of a need. There is no conflict on our planet at the level of needs. We all have the same needs. The problem is in strategies for meeting the needs.
>
> —Marshall Rosenberg

As a general rule for figuring out if something is a need or a strategy, ask yourself, "Can everyone have this at the same time?" If not, it's not a need but a strategy. Dig deeper to find the need.

> **Rule of Thumb**
>
> If everyone cannot have it at once, it's a strategy, not a need. Dig deeper to find the real need.

Years back, when I was first learning about Marshall Rosenberg's work, I attended a workshop where we learned to differentiate between needs and strategies. At the time, I was having a lot of conflict with a family member, and I asked the facilitator for help in understanding what this person's needs might be when we get into arguments. "It seems to me that they feel a need to be right," I said.

"But everyone can't be right," the instructor explained. "Being right is a strategy . . . what might the need be?" After thinking more, I saw that maybe being right was this person's way of feeling important, knowing that they matter, or feeling capable. Immediately, I felt more compassion toward them because I understood those needs. I have them, too. That experience was a powerful one for healing my family relationship, and I have seen similar changes happen when people use this way of thinking to understand and resolve financial conflicts.

Maria and Martin's Story Maria loved scrapbooking, and was buying so many craft items that it had become a source of conflict between her and her husband, Martin. He saw the expense as frivolous, but she couldn't put a price on how the creative act of scrapbooking made her feel. The hobby met her needs for connection to her loved ones, creative expression, beauty, fun, and meaning, but the tension with her husband threatened her needs for peace and intimacy. Martin loved seeing Maria happy, but being on a fixed income, he worried about any unnecessary spending. When Maria, who already had a bureau full of craft items, came home with new ones, it threatened Martin's needs for security and peace of mind. He knew that this one hobby wouldn't ruin their retirement plans, but to Martin it felt wasteful to spend on non-necessities. Maria didn't *need* to buy more scrapbooking items.

Her continued spending in this area felt to him like an act of disrespect toward all of his hard work and his values. Why couldn't she be a little more practical?

Maria knew that she didn't *need* more craft materials, but those that she had were not inspiring to her because she had already used all of those patterns and shapes. Part of the adventure of scrapbooking for Maria was searching for items that she could turn into a new creation. She scrimped and saved in other ways, and it was difficult for her to understand why her husband would begrudge her this simple pleasure in life. To her, his resistance felt like an insult, and an act of disrespect toward all of her hard work and sacrifice over their years together. Why couldn't he just let her have some fun? The argument had gone on for years, and both Martin and Maria felt sure it would never be resolved.

Then, Maria learned the difference between a need and a strategy. By recognizing that the hunt for new scrapbooking items was meeting needs for fun and creative expression, she started to brainstorm how she could meet those same needs without threatening Martin's need for security. She was beaming when she announced her idea: She would host a scrapbook swap. Surely she was not the only one with a wealth of unused items.

Now, every so often, Maria's dining room becomes a virtual store full of new shapes and colors to browse, and every one of them has a story to go with it from a friend who has already used that pattern in a project. Maria's needs for adventure and creativity are completely satisfied by this strategy, and Martin finds it extremely practical, filling him with a feeling of security and peace. Now, when Maria shows Martin one of her pieces, he sees the pictures instead of a price tag. Sharing treasured memories, lovingly preserved by Maria, adds to their intimacy rather than creating tension.

Maria and Martin's situation may seem petty in comparison with your own. I assure you, it was not petty to them. When an argument spans multiple years, the buildup of resentment and sensitivity can turn a small disagreement into a seemingly insurmountable challenge. I see this quite often when couples are mismatched in their financial strategies. Arguments arise over the strategies each person uses, but rarely do people understand how to dig deeper and talk about the needs they are each meeting with those strategies. Learning to communicate about needs opens the door for true resolution and understanding. We are not seeking compromise. What we are looking for is a solution where both people are completely satisfied with the outcome.

Tendai and Dunya Tendai and Dunya had been married for several years before their financial conflicts surfaced. Dunya was the daughter of immigrants who had struggled to put food on the table, and her experience made her determined to save, in the hope that she would have more comfort in her adult life. Having money in the bank made Dunya feel secure and safe, and she loved watching the numbers in her saving accounts grow. The more savings she had, the more secure she felt in the knowledge that she would never again have to live with the stress that had filled her childhood. To Dunya, saving money met her needs for security and peace of mind.

Tendai had also grown up in a modest household, but his emotional response to money was very different. Having felt for years that he was missing out on some of life's best pleasures for lack of money, he associated money with freedom and adventure. When he graduated college and began working in the finance industry, his salary finally allowed him to begin experiencing all he had dreamed of as a child. Tendai used his extra money to travel, go to concerts and the theater, dress elegantly, and live in an affluent neighborhood. For the first few years of their marriage, even though they pooled their resources in a shared bank account, Tendai and Dunya always had enough slack in their finances to meet Dunya's need for security and Tendai's need for freedom. There were occasional disagreements about priorities, but they were fairly inconsequential. Then the Great Recession hit, and Tendai was laid off.

They began to cut back on spending in the months that followed. They no longer traveled. They canceled their concert hall and theater memberships. Tendai cooked for them at home rather than eating out.

All of this helped them to pay their mortgage and regular expenses without draining their savings very much.

As the duration of unemployment grew longer, both Tendai and Dunya grew more anxious. Dunya feared that their savings would not last. Images of her childhood frequently crossed her mind, and as she watched their savings account balance erode, she began to feel a sense of desperation growing in her belly. She started to clip coupons and cut costs wherever she could. This had a negative effect on Tendai. Their financial strain also reminded him of his uncomfortable childhood, but instead of triggering a desire for security as it did with Dunya, it heightened his desire for freedom. He had already stopped doing so many of the things that he loved, and watching Dunya clip coupons reminded him of his mother and the stress she carried with her when he was a child. This filled him with feelings of anger and desperation. He sought solace in small luxuries like a gourmet cappuccino or a new tie. Dunya found these small extravagances extremely irresponsible. The more she argued for him to rein in his spending, the more it triggered Tendai's deep fears of missing out on life. The more he argued that life wasn't worth living without some small pleasures, the more afraid she became that his actions would destroy the little security they had left. The arguments became more frequent and more heated, to the point where this conflict threatened the foundation of their relationship.

Thankfully, Tendai found work, bringing a temporary reprieve to the conflict. However, when Dunya discovered she was pregnant, the issue was brought back to the fore. Dunya wanted to stay home with their child for the first few years, and she feared that the loss of her income combined with the increased costs of living with a child would bring them to the brink of divorce once again. Tendai did not want to raise his children under the same cloud of stress that he had experienced. He feared that Dunya's anxiety about saving would again interfere with his happiness, even though he was no longer unemployed. They had plenty of money, and they were on track for a comfortable retirement even without Dunya's income. He saw her fears as overblown, while she thought he was being flippant and unrealistic about the need to be prepared for any crisis. The prospect of a child intensified each person's fears. Old arguments arose even while Dunya was still working. There seemed to be no way to resolve their different financial priorities. Both were responding to fears of reliving their uncomfortable pasts, but their different perspectives came from the separate needs that each one had learned to meet with money.

These types of conflicts remind me of the Fourth Circle of Hell from Dante's *Divine Comedy.* In this realm, hoarders and wasters are together condemned to perpetually push against boulders that collide with one another. The people who led lives of prodigality, loosely spending all they had, push from one side, shouting to the others, "Why do you hoard?" On the other side, those who had held tightly to all they could get push their own rocks up against the others, crying, "Why do you waste?" The conflict is doomed to rage on for eternity with neither side making any progress.[3] When I meet couples where one is a spender and one is a saver, I immediately hear a chorus shouting, "Why do you hoard? Why do you waste?" in my mind.

When two people have financial conflict, the disagreement is really about how they are using their resources to meet their needs. As long as the conversation is focused on strategies, the conflict will continue. If, on the other hand, you can learn to identify the needs that are in play, the conversation can become more productive. Remember, needs are universal. Once you understand the need someone is trying to meet, even if their strategy seems wrong or misguided, you will be able to identify with some part of their motive because you have the same needs as they do. In Tendai and Dunya's case, rather than focus on, "Why do you hoard?" and "Why do you waste?," which are both strategies, a more productive conversation would be to ask, "Why does saving feel so good to you?," "What is it about these little extravagances that lights you up so much?," or "What are you afraid will happen if you didn't do that?" An even better tactic might be to pull out the list of needs from the worksheet section in the back of this book, and point to the needs that your particular strategy meets for you. Then, you can talk together about why that need feels so important in that particular situation. Once you both feel heard and understood, you can begin to explore strategies that will work for *both* of you.

From my own experience, and talking with many others, it would seem that when money is tight, it turns up the volume on particular needs, but which needs shout louder will be unique to the individual. For Sylvia, who lived with the insecurity of knowing that her husband could be laid off again any moment, her needs for beauty and comfort were triggered when money got tight. For Dunya, it was her need for security. For Tendai, his needs for freedom and adventure cried out when he limited his travel and exposure to the arts and cultural activities. When couples merge their lives together, their economies also blend. That means that the strategies for resource management need to satisfy both people's needs or else there will be discomfort, dissatisfaction, and conflict. The goal is not to compromise on which needs are met, but to compromise on strategies so that all needs are met. Conflict happens when our strategy to meet one set of needs interferes with other needs being met.

It is easy to see how strategies can conflict when two people are involved, but it happens all the time within our lives as individuals as well. Quite often, an attempt to meet one of our needs will directly conflict with another of our own needs. Most often, I see this when people's strategies for meeting their immediate needs for comfort or fun stand in the way of their need for long-term security. They spend all they have today because they feel entitled to some comfort and reward for their hard work, but because of this they have little savings, no long-term plan, and no roadmap for ever being able to stop working and really live comfortably.

Getting ahead is not about getting ahead of *other people*. This is important. Financial independence is about getting ahead of our own needs, and building strategies that will satisfy us today while also meeting our needs for long-term stability so that when we are no longer able to labor, all our needs will still be satisfied. Living paycheck to paycheck is like treading water: you are surviving, but not moving forward. When you start to develop savings, you are effectively getting out in front of your future needs. You are a step ahead of life's expenses.

To get ahead, we have to find strategies that allow us to spend less than we earn so we can build up assets other than labor. Otherwise, we will have no income when we stop working.[4] We do this by first assessing our current strategies, and then looking for areas where we can put our resources to better use to meet more needs and generate fewer expenses at the same time. I call this process *needs mapping*, and it will help you build a budget that feels easy, and satisfying, to keep.

Needs Mapping

The simple fact that so many people feel uncomfortably restricted by the idea of a budget is evidence that the budgets we are used to creating are not ideal for us. If the idea of a budget, or your current budget, feels restrictive, that means that on some level, living by that plan threatens one or more of your needs. If you hate the idea of setting limits, it might be your need for freedom. If you are disappointed that your budget doesn't allow for eating out as much as you would like, it could be your needs for connection, fun, relaxation, or even adventure or esteem that are threatened. Regardless of which needs are threatened by your budget, the fact that a budget feels uncomfortable is a problem. If you do not love your financial plan, you will be consistently fighting against it. We want peace in our financial lives, not chronic conflict.

Needs mapping begins with the expenses column from your Cash Flow worksheet. In the same way that you traced each of your income streams back to the resources that produce them, now take stock of the needs you are currently meeting with your money by tracing every expense back to the need or needs being served. By doing this, two things will start to become apparent. First, you should start to see some themes emerge that help you to identify which needs are most important to you, and which ones you are using money for to meet most often. Second, you may find yourself feeling more appreciative and grateful for your bills. Early on in my adult life, I struggled with resentment when I paid my bills. I hated handing over my hard-earned (and very limited) cash to pay for things that I barely thought about, like electricity. When I started to practice needs mapping, I began to understand that electricity didn't just meet my need for ease or light, but also for beauty, connection, comfort, communication, learning, and on and on. The list of activities I can enjoy and environments I can create because of electricity and electronics is nearly endless. When I pay my electric bill now, I think about the coziness of dimmed lights inside on a chilly evening or the relief of air conditioning on a sweltering day. When I pay the water bill, I think about hot bubble baths and refreshing showers. When I pay my phone bill, I think about the people I love and the conversations we've shared recently, or the times my GPS has helped me find my way around in a strange city. The money I spend is never in vain. It always serves a need, and this knowledge builds a deep sense of gratitude and satisfaction for all that I am able to enjoy because of my money, even as I write checks to part with some of it.

To illustrate, we'll follow along with a very simple example. People frequently come to me to ask for help with their budgets. I always ask them to bring me a list of all of their regular expenses and all of their sources of income, and we start with their Cash Flow. For example, Raphael is a recent college graduate who shares a house with several other single folks in a mid-sized U.S. city. His parents paid for his education, so he has no significant debt. His goal is to save $12,000 for a period of extended international travel. Figure 4.10 shows the Cash Flow we built with the information he brought to me.

Income	Expenses	
2600	650	Rent
	75	Utilities
	150	Food
	400	Going Out
	200	Everything Else
2600	1475	
Saving	$1125	
Goal	$750	

Figure 4.10   Raphael's Cash Flow

Once this basic Cash Flow was outlined, we considered what was missing. In Raphael's case, I knew he had a car, yet there was nothing on his Cash Flow sheet that would suggest this. I used the needs list to help him think through the types of things he regularly spends money on, but doesn't think about often enough to call to mind easily. Not only did he remember the car and all of the expenses associated with it, but his yoga practice, digital subscriptions, and money he spends on entertainment and socializing all came to mind after thinking through the Needs List. Raphael isn't absentminded or ignorant about his money. Most of us have expenses that we forget to budget for. The Needs List can help you to think through all of the less obvious expenses that arise from time to time. Gifts for friends, personal development books, music and video downloads, in-app purchases, taxes, and online subscriptions are just a few of the things that people tend to leave out when they list their expenses from memory. The Needs List can help you make a more comprehensive record of actual expenses.

The full list of Raphael's initial expenses, with estimates for average monthly amounts for those items that come up only once in a while, is shown in Figure 4.11.

I also suggest adding an "everything else" item as a buffer for your monthly budget. Most of us have a certain number of unexpected costs that arise from time to time, yet I've noticed people do not tend to budget for this. Over time, you will come to see how large your buffer should be. This will depend on your lifestyle and situation. I generally recommend that an average family budget at least $400 to $500 per month as a buffer. This is different from your emergency fund since it covers nonemergencies like unexpected copays on prescriptions, buying a gift for a wedding, a broken arm, or sponsoring a friend in a fundraising effort.

Emergency savings is a crucial part of any financial plan. Unfortunately, we have a savings crisis in the United States. You may recall from the first section of this book that 70 percent of American adults are moderately or severely stressed about money, and according to a study by the National Bureau of Economic Research, nearly half of Americans say they could not come up with $2,000 in 30 days if they

Strategy				Strategy
	Income	Expenses		
Desk Job at				
Wildlife Org	2600	650	Rent	
		75	Util	
		40	Car ($\frac{1}{2}$ parents)	
		150	Food	
		0	Phone (parents)	
		75	Yoga	
		300	Lunch	
		320	Bars	
		160	Restaurants	
		300	Entertainment	
		60	Taxi	
		200	Buffer	
	2600	2330		
	Saving	**$270**		
	Goal	**$750**		
	Left to Find	$480		

Current Savings	$3,000
Savings Goal	$12,000
Months till goal	12
Monthly Goal	$750

Figure 4.11   Raphael's Real Cash Flow

needed to.[5] Your emergency fund is there to help you if you are faced with large, unexpected expenses. If your car breaks down, your water heater needs to be replaced, or you have to fly to see a dying relative on a moment's notice, your emergency fund should cover that.

In general, it is a good practice to have three to six months' worth of savings in your emergency fund, but the number varies depending on your situation. The logic behind this number is simple. If you were to lose your job, how long would it take you to find another position that is as good or better than your current one? For some, it would be very quick, and for others it could take a very long time. This is why so many executives have severance packages built into their employment contracts. It can take an incredibly long time, sometimes several years, to secure a C-level position. An executive severance package ensures that the person can afford to take the time to find other work at the same level. If you are not able to secure a severance package, your emergency fund serves that purpose. If you are wondering how much you need in your own emergency fund, a colleague of mine developed a free online calculator to help you estimate the amount you should save.[6] The amount you need may be much larger than you expect, but having a fully funded emergency fund is one of the critical steps in getting ahead financially. Investing the months or years of savings to build up this fund is well worth your while.

A truly satisfying financial plan is one that allows you to meet your current needs *and* to set aside money for your future needs. As I've said before, getting ahead is not about getting ahead of other people. What we want is to get ahead of ourselves. Getting ahead means you are ahead of *your own* expenses. You may know what it feels like to fall behind on bills or carry a lot of debt. I know from experience that it is a very unpleasant way to live. Getting ahead isn't about having a better TV or car than your neighbor. Those are strategies to meet needs for respect, esteem, or knowing you matter, and they can be very costly and ineffective ways to meet those needs. Getting ahead is not about competing, but rather the feeling of peace and satisfaction that comes with knowing you can meet all of your needs, now and tomorrow, with your own resources.

Once you have a full list of all of your expenses and the needs they serve, you can start to do the real work. We start with our current strategies and needs, and then we can adjust the strategies, if necessary, to meet more needs with fewer expenses.

To try this yourself, use the Expenses and Needs Worksheet in Appendix B. Make a simple list of your expenses in the Expenses column, and then for each expense, look down the list of needs and take note of which ones (material and nonmaterial) that expense serves. The thing to notice here is just how many nonphysical needs you are meeting with your expenses. In some cases, this is good news. If your home meets your needs for beauty, social connection, and peace as well as your physical needs for shelter and security, you may feel grateful and happy about that. On the other hand, if you are seeing that a lot of your expenses map only to esteem needs or other "higher-order" needs, that is an opportunity to fine-tune your strategies.

You now have a map of all the financial strategies you currently use to meet your needs. From here, you can start to ask yourself some important questions. Are these strategies working well? Are the needs you are meeting truly satisfied, or still lacking? Are you happy with the ratio of physical and nonphysical needs in your financial strategies? And, of course, when you look at all of your financial strategies, including saving for emergencies and long-term security, can you afford them?

When I work with people on their budgeting plans, it is rare that they have more than enough income to meet all of their spending and savings goals without a bit of reorganization. Otherwise, why would they have sought out budgeting help in the first place? If, after taking stock of all of your needs and expenses, including the needs for security (saving for the future), you have more income available to you, then you will not need to do the following exercises. If, on the other hand, your expenses exceed your income, or you want to fine-tune your plan so that you can save more or pay down debt faster, then they will help you get there. The purpose of these activities is to get you to start creative problem-solving on the level of needs. Just as you did with your Resources List—brainstorming how you could increase income by creatively employing your unused resources—here you will think about how to reduce your expenses by meeting needs with nonfinancial strategies. In the next section we will tie all of these concepts together and build a full plan that incorporates resources, assets, income, expenses, liabilities, and needs.

Exercises: Needs

In the same way that you used the Resources List to brainstorm how to creatively build assets, now we'll do the same with needs. Listed next are two ideas for

(Continued)

(*Continued*)

how you can use the Needs List to strengthen different financial skills. It may sound simplistic or silly, but these exercises are fun ways to challenge your current ways of thinking about how you meet your needs.

1. Write each need from the Expenses & Needs List on an index card. Then, mix them up and draw one Needs card at random. Think of three ways you can meet this need without spending *any* money.

Coming up with ideas for how to meet our needs with nonfinancial strategies is extremely useful, but it is important to do this *before* you find yourself in a situation where you might be tempted to spend for emotional reasons. By simply listing several ways you might meet a certain need without money, you are arming yourself with new options that you can bring to mind any time you feel tempted to fall back into a financial strategy when that particular need is triggered. Thinking of new strategies in the heat of the moment is hard. Remembering ideas you already thought through is easy.

2. Draw three Needs cards at random. Devise one strategy to meet all three needs.

This activity can be extremely practical or very silly depending on how you approach it. I recommend opting for silly first, and then moving into the more practical. The purpose of the exercise is to break out of habitual thinking patterns, so the more absurd you can get, the more creative you will find yourself becoming, and this will help when it comes to devising real and practical strategies.

Rules of Thumb for Creative Resource Management

As you begin to brainstorm new strategies for maximizing the income potential of your resources and minimizing the expenses generated by your needs, you will be faced with many kinds of tradeoffs. Should you carpool to work or ride the train? In some cases, you will find nonfinancial strategies can be just as satisfying or more so than financial ones. Sometimes, a financial strategy is completely necessary, but the tradeoffs can be difficult to weigh (should you take out a loan to buy a car, or not?). In the cases where it is necessary or desired to use a financial strategy, there are some simple rules of thumb, based on the concepts we've already discussed, that can help you make financially sound and beneficial choices. This section will give you a brief overview of them, and explain how they can help you simplify otherwise complex financial decisions.

Remember that when it comes to your day-to-day money management, you can think of assets and liabilities like this: *If it earns more money than it costs, it's an asset. If it costs more than it earns, it's a liability.* I call this the Asset Test, and this simple little definition can take you a long way toward financial stability.

The Asset Test

Will it earn me more than it costs?

Consider a car. Many people think of a car as an asset, but let's look at a car through the lens of these definitions. A car certainly has financial value. It can be sold or rented. Technically, a car would qualify as physical capital in economic terms. A car might get you to work to earn your paycheck, and it may save you time and energy when compared with public transportation. It's no wonder so many people think of their car as an asset. Nevertheless, a car has at least seven, and sometimes more, expense items associated with it:

1. Insurance
2. Fuel
3. Maintenance
4. Parking
5. Excise tax
6. Registration fees
7. Inspection fees

Not to mention loan payments (if you financed), car washes, paying tolls, possible parking or speeding tickets, roadside assistance, and the fact that a car is always *losing* resale value as it gets older. So, I ask you: Is a car an asset or a liability? Usually, a car is a liability.

Of course, there are exceptions. If you own a collector's car in great condition, you might be able to sell it for more than it cost. If you drive for Uber or Lyft in your free time, or you put it in a car share and charge other people to drive it while you're at work, then maybe it will earn you more than it costs. Still, you can see how the simple definitions of assets and liabilities makes quick work of deciding if something is a drain on your income or a source of income. And remember, just because something is a liability doesn't mean you have to eliminate it from your life. A car might be an important source of convenience or joy for you. Our task is not to eliminate all liabilities and expenses, but simply to make sure that every liability can be met through the income from our assets.

We often hear that a college education is a good investment, but these definitions can help us see when that is true and when it isn't. While it's true that, on average, people with a college degree earn much more over their lifetime than people without one, that doesn't mean that a college degree is always an asset, especially when you consider its price tag. If you complete a couple of years, financing your studies with loans, and then decide you want to travel the world, is that education an asset? No. You will have higher expenses after you leave because your loans will come due with interest, but you won't have gained the ability to earn more than you could have before you started because you didn't finish the degree. Your experiences may have been "priceless," but the tuition still has to be paid.

For some professions, a degree is mandatory and the salary you can expect after graduation is much greater than what you could earn without a higher education. With other lines of work, you may be better off training as an apprentice under a skilled expert, or starting out in an entry-level position and working your way up. How do you know which will be best for you in the long run? You have to think about the potential income and the total costs, and decide which is affordable for your situation. You certainly need *skills*, but you don't necessarily need college.

Using the Asset Test, many things that are technically defined as assets (mostly those in the physical capital category) turn out to be liabilities. Your clothes, your furniture, your tools, and your jewelry are all things that have resale value, and so they technically qualify as assets. In reality, though, most of these things would not be able to be sold for *more* than the price you originally paid, and so when all is said and done, they are a drain on your income. Again, they are not worthless or items to be discarded just because they aren't assets. The point here is to understand which items in your life put you in a stronger financial situation when you buy them, and which ones erode your bottom line.

Avoiding Common Financial Mistakes with the Asset Test

The Asset Test can also help to explain some of the more confusing parts of the credit system.

Good and Bad Debt When you borrow money, there is a difference between "good debt" and "bad debt." Good debt doesn't damage your credit score, and the interest is often tax deductible. Bad debt can hurt your credit score, making it harder to borrow in the future, and there are no tax benefits for the interest you pay. There are two things that generally qualify as good debt: education loans and home loans. Why is this debt "good"? Because when you borrow money to get a degree or to buy property, you are investing in *assets*. A degree usually increases the value of your labor, making your potential income stream larger. A home loan buys you land, which has many potential income streams associated with it. In both of these cases, you are borrowing money to increase your income potential. These purchases often put you in a better financial position than you were in when you started, which is why they don't hurt your credit score and the government is willing to give you a tax break on the interest.

When you borrow money to buy *stuff*, you almost always end up in a worse financial position than when you started. If you buy something on credit and don't pay it off immediately, you pay interest on that purchase. By the time you've paid it off, that item will be worth less than when you bought it because it is used. On top of that, you will have paid more for it than it was worth in the first place.

> **Rule of Thumb**
>
> It's generally okay to borrow money to buy *assets*, but not for *liabilities*.

Borrowing money to buy things that lose their value or are immediately consumed, and then paying interest on the money you borrowed, is not a smart financial move. That's why this type of debt is considered "bad." Car loans, boat loans, credit cards, and store cards all fall under the category of "consumer debt," and this kind of borrowing is almost always bad for you in the long run. Again, it may be worth paying the interest, but you have to really think carefully before borrowing money to buy something that doesn't earn you more than you're paying.

Exceptions and Grey Areas Of course, every rule has its exceptions, and we can't always know ahead of time whether something will grow or shrink in value. Sometimes, when we buy something, we're *speculating* on its future value. When someone buys shares of stock, for example, there is no way of knowing for certain whether the price will go up or down. Homes historically rise in value, but anyone who lived through the housing crisis of the early 2000s knows this is not always the case. Anything you buy in the *hopes* that it will increase in value is speculation, and when it comes to speculation, take caution.

When it comes to speculation, you're taking a risk, so make sure that you have good reason for thinking that the value will increase. If you are borrowing to fund a business, how certain are you that there is a market for what you are selling? If you are borrowing to prototype an invention, how committed are you to selling the patent or creating a company when you've completed the project? I don't recommend borrowing to buy highly speculative things like stock, but even paying for stock in cash is speculative, and you should examine your reasons for believing it will increase in value before you buy it.

Even school loans and home loans have an element of speculation. If you are borrowing to go to college, how sure are you that
you will finish? If you are borrowing to buy a house, how solid is
the foundation? What is the history of the neighborhood, and what
are the community's plans for the future? The Asset Test makes life
simpler, but it doesn't replace sitting down and thinking things
through.

Good and Bad Credit Do not confuse good and bad *debt* with good
and bad *credit*. The type of debt you have depends on what you borrow the money for. The type of credit you have depends on how
dependable you are in paying back what you owe. You can have
excellent credit and bad debt. You can have terrible credit and good
debt. Ideally, you will have good credit and good debt, but should
you avoid debt altogether?

Rule of Thumb

Good or bad debt depends on what you borrow. Good or bad credit depends on
your repayment history.

A lot of people I talk to have avoided credit cards because they have
been taught that they are terrible consumer traps. This can be true, but
if you want to build a strong financial life, should you avoid all types of
credit? No, you should not. In fact, unless you believe you don't have
the self-control to have a credit card and *not use it*, you should most
definitely have some sort of loan or credit on file. Why? Because without it, banks and other lenders will have no way of knowing if you can
be trusted to pay back what you borrow. Having no history of borrowing money and paying it back can hurt you down the line when you
want to borrow money to buy an asset like a home. Lenders base important decisions on your borrowing history, and they determine your
borrowing history by using your credit score. In order to have a credit
score, you need to have a credit history.

Your Credit Score When a lender gives out money, they risk not getting it back. If you've borrowed money and paid it back on time in the past, then lending to you is less of a risk for them. How do they determine how much of a risk you are? They use your credit score.

Your credit score is a number between about 300 and 850, and it is a fast way for lenders to learn if you can be relied on to repay what you borrow. If you have no credit history, lenders may not lend to you at all, or if they do they will charge you a much higher interest rate than they would if you had a good credit score. Your credit score is based on your credit report.

Getting your credit report is easy. Every American is entitled to one free copy per year of their credit report. This report shows all of your loan accounts, credit cards, store cards, and the like. Getting your credit report every year is a good idea for several reasons. First, you can check to make sure that it is accurate. A recent report by the Federal Trade Commission[7] estimated that 20 percent of Americans—one out of every five people—have inaccuracies on their credit reports. In some of these cases, the errors are small and easily resolved. Sometimes, though, the mistakes are major and can even point to identity fraud if someone is using your personal information to open credit accounts. Even though the credit-reporting agencies track your financial life, it is not their responsibility to make sure the reports are accurate. If there is an error on your credit report, it is *your* responsibility to contact the credit agencies and get it resolved.

Getting your score is easy, too. Some credit card companies give you a periodic update on your score as a perk of having an account with them. If you don't have access to this service, check out the Consumer Financial Protection Bureau's (CFPB) article on ways to access your score.[8] The CFPB is a government group that exists to protect people from predatory financial practices, so you can trust their advice.

Building Good Credit without Bad Debt Good credit is important if you want to borrow, but remember that borrowing money is usually only wise if you borrow to buy an *asset*. How, then, do you build a good credit score without getting yourself into bad debt?

One way is to borrow only for things considered good debt. Education loans can be a great way to establish credit if you plan well. If you are a U.S. citizen, you are eligible for federal education loans even if you have no credit history. It's one way that the government tries to help people build their financial situation. Still, even though college loans are considered good debt, they can become an incredible burden if you are training for a low-paying job. Again, you have to think of the Asset Test. Will an education earn you more than it costs you? How certain are you that you will finish what you started and graduate? Will your starting salary after graduation be enough to cover your living expenses plus the loan payments? One rule of thumb for student loans is that you don't want to borrow more than you expect to earn in your first year after graduation. A quick dive into Salary.com or GlassDoor.com can give you an idea of how starting salaries vary for different jobs. If you plan to study art or social work, you can expect to reach your max loan limit much sooner than your friend who is studying engineering or nursing. Don't assume that because you *can* take out more in loans for school that you *should*. Borrowing money for an education is only a good idea if that education will allow you to earn back more than you borrowed. Otherwise, your degree is not an asset but a very expensive piece of paper.

Rule of Thumb

Your total school loans should not be more than your expected first year's salary after graduation.

Another way to build good credit is to apply for a credit card and *never carry a balance*. This is especially easy to manage if you already pay a bill or two using automatic debits from your bank account. For example, if you pay your phone bill automatically from your checking account, set it up instead to be paid by your credit card. Then, set up a payment in the same amount from your bank account to the credit card a day or two later. In this way, you will be using the card (which is important because inactive accounts often get closed by the credit card company, and that can hurt your score instead of helping it), but you will never be paying interest. It's a little bit of a hassle to get everything set up and automated, but once you do you'll be building a credit history with almost no effort. Be careful, though: For some people, just having access to credit is just too tempting. If you want to use a credit card but you don't want to take it shopping, it's best to keep that card hidden away in a file or cut it up after you set your automatic payments. You know yourself better than anyone. Only you can decide if you can handle having a credit card without getting yourself into debt.

Having credit and not using it is the second most important factor in calculating your credit score. Your *utilization* rate is the amount of money you owe on an account divided by the total amount you could borrow from them. So if you have a credit card with a $1,000 credit line and you owe $500, your utilization rate is 50 percent.

Lenders want to know that you can have access to money without using it all. Having a low utilization rate shows that you can handle the temptation of credit and keep your spending to reasonable levels. While it's best to pay off your debts *in full*, if you are going to carry a balance on your credit accounts, you should try to keep your utilization rate below 30 percent.

Rule of Thumb

Don't let your balance go above 30 percent of your available credit.

After learning about this rule, a woman in one of my workshops decided to reorganize her credit card debt so that she could improve her credit score. She had one card with a high utilization rate and others with low ones. She decided that she would transfer the balance from the card with the high utilization rate to one of the others in order to have less than 30 percent on all of her credit card accounts.

Before she did this, though, she decided to call the credit card company and tell them what she was planning to do. Since she was a good customer and paid her bills on time they didn't want to lose her business to another card, so they *raised her credit limit* to the point where her current balance was less than 30 percent of her credit line. This boosted her credit score without her having to move her balance to another account. It also raised her overall available credit limit, so her score was improved in two ways.

A good credit score can help you save tens of thousands of dollars in interest on a mortgage. It can help you get approved for an apartment lease, and even help you get a job, since employers are looking at credit scores more and more often. These are some pretty big payoffs. However, some credit cards charge high annual fees and very high interest rates. If you don't trust yourself to have access to money without spending it, credit cards are probably not a good choice for you. If this all sounds confusing, just go back to the Asset Rule. Credit, when used well, can be a great asset by costing you very little and boosting your credit score. On the other hand, if not managed well, credit can quickly become an enormous liability. Only you know yourself well enough to decide which is which for you.

Putting It in All Together: Your Personal Economy

We have now explored money management in three different ways. We looked at income and expenses, assets and liabilities, and finally, resources and needs. These three perspectives correspond to three different but interconnected models of money management.

Budgeting usually focuses only on the Cash Flow component of money management (income and expenses), but as you now know, there is a lot more to the story. Accountants and financial advisors often think about assets and liabilities, but even that is incomplete. What we are really talking about when we talk about money is *personal economics.* Each of us has our own private economy that we manage, to our own benefit or detriment. I like to call this your *personal economy* because it is an illustration of how you are directing your unique set of resources to meet your personal needs.

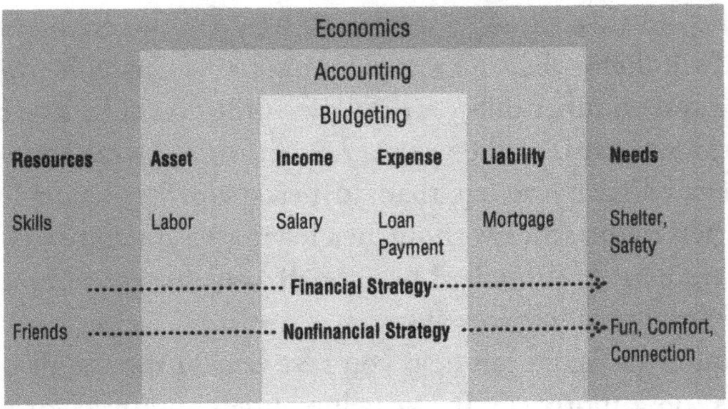

Figure 4.12   Personal Economics

The concept map in Figure 4.12 shows how all three models of money management fit together to create our personal economy. Up to this point, we have talked about these concepts separately, but now we will use all of these concepts together to develop a personal financial plan that can get you to your specific financial goals without compromising your needs along the way. The task here is to start from your current situation, take stock of your resources and your needs, and then see how you can adjust your plan in order to maximize the income you are creating with your resources and minimize the expenses that are generated by your needs. We will start with a simple example and walk through each step of optimizing a personal economy. After this illustration, you will have the challenge—and the opportunity— to go through this process with your own finances and build a plan for your personal economy.

It's important to note that, while some financial advisors will say that there is an "ideal" breakdown of how much you spend on certain categories (30 percent on housing, 10 percent or less on debt, 15 percent toward saving, etc.) your personal economic plan should meet *your* needs and your priorities, or else it will feel uncomfortable and you will not stick to it. Also, some areas of the world have very different costs of living. To say that you should have your total housing costs stay under 30 percent of your after-tax income may be fine if you live in the suburbs or a rural area, but in some of the more expensive cities that is quite unrealistic for most people. The 30 percent rule is standard because that is the amount of housing costs that lenders use to decide if you can afford a loan. It may be a good rule of thumb, but in some places it is not realistic. In cities like San Francisco and New York, it is common to spend 40 percent or more on housing. The purpose is to direct your resources to your needs in such a way that you personally feel satisfied, and the ratios of categories can vary depending on your personality and your environment.

A colleague of mine recently made an interesting observation about financial priorities in different cities, and his comments made me think about how our neighborhoods can affect the strategies we use to meet our needs. This colleague has lived in three major American cities in the last few years. He noticed that in one city, people spend a lot of money to live in a neighborhood where they have a decent commute to work and the school systems are good. Housing is a major expense due to location in that city. In another city, people have very small homes that are not conducive to entertaining, so they spend a lot more money going out to eat with friends. In the third city, it is very cold, so people make their homes a place for living and socializing. Having nice furniture and lots of entertainment options is a priority there. He noticed that in each place he has lived, he has felt a pull to spend money in different categories based on the culture of the city and the people there. This just reinforced for me the belief that there is no set percentage of a person's income that "should" go to one category or another. While there are some good guidelines, there is no magic proportion. Your economic priorities should be set based on your current and future needs.

Putting all of the concepts we've discussed so far together, it's time to start building your personal economic plan. For illustration purposes, we will continue to follow along with Raphael, a recent graduate in his mid-twenties who wanted to increase his monthly savings to save up for an adventure abroad. Raphael and I created a Cash Flow sheet (Figure 4.13) to look at how he was currently directing his resources. That Cash Flow is repeated here.

Strategy			Strategy
	Income	Expenses	
Desk Job at Wildlife Org	2600	650	Rent
		75	Util
		40	Car ($\frac{1}{2}$ parents)
		150	Food
		0	Phone (parents)
		75	Yoga
		300	Lunch
		320	Bars
		160	Restaurants
		300	Entertainment
		60	Taxi
		200	Buffer
	2600	2330	
	Saving	**$270**	
	Goal	**$750**	
	Left to Find	$480	

Current Saving's	$3,000
Savings Goal	$12,000
Months till goal	12
Monthly Goal	$750

Figure 4.13   Raphael's Actual Cash Flow

Once we had this, we could start to look at the strategies Raphael was using to optimize his personal economy and reach his goal. Specifically, he wanted to save $12,000 in one year's time. He already had $3,000 saved and he was living very inexpensively by renting a room in a large house with several friends. Still, he knew that there was more he could do to save because, as low as his expenses were, he felt as if his money disappeared every month. He couldn't explain this based on his budgeted expenses, so he looked back into his bank records to see where all his money had gone over the past couple of months. Many banks and applications have tools to help you track your spending and see what categories you put the most money toward. These can be very useful in helping you to figure out which of your needs you tend to serve the most with your money. In Raphael's case, he was surprised to see how much he spent on takeout food. He ate breakfast and lunch away from home every weekday, and often ate dinner at restaurants as well. There was a lot of room to be creative in the food category, so we started by looking at these behaviors and expenses in light of his needs.

Raphael's first instinct was to say, "I'll just stop ordering takeout," but I urged him to slow down and think that through. Yes, we needed to cut some food expenses, but first we needed to figure out what needs he was meeting with his current behavior. As we talked, it became clear that the only thing that got Raphael out of bed and into the office in the mornings was the thought of a croissant and coffee on his way to work. Clearly this was not an area to cut because he would have to rearrange the most difficult part of his day (he is not a morning person). We wanted to find a money-saving strategy that he would embrace, not fight against. Eating out in the evenings was socially motivated, and he didn't tend to pack a lunch because he hadn't made food the night before. He would gladly cook at home when he was with friends, but cooking alone often felt like a pain after a long day. After some discussion around daily habits, and the reasons behind them (social connection, convenience, etc.), Raphael had a solid plan to change his food spending and eating behaviors:

- ► Two or three times a week, he would cook dinner with his room-mates or invite a friend over to cook together.
- ► While cooking with friends, he would make extra portions and pack them for lunches.

Raphael felt sure that this strategy would be an improvement over his current behavior—not only would it save him money, but it would also improve on the quality of his social time. He would still go out, but he would limit his restaurant meals to mostly weekends.

This helped him find a good chunk of cash to save, but not quite enough. This is when we turned to the Resources column. Raphael's day job is not his passion. He tolerates his desk job by dreaming of saving enough money to go teach English in Vietnam. His real passions are music and wrestling, and he is incredibly talented at both. Raphael decided that if he was going to have friends over a couple of nights per week to cook and play music, his social life would be satisfied enough that he could invest a few evenings per month giving music lessons or teaching his neighbor how to wrestle. In his area, and with his skill level, he could easily earn $50 an hour teaching guitar, so he decided to try to give two lessons per month. He already had been approached by one person for lessons, and had an idea of where to find other students. Wrestling, on the other hand, he wanted to teach pro bono. His neighbor could not afford the lessons, but knowing how much wrestling had helped his own self-esteem in high school, Raphael wanted to give that gift to this boy. This strategy didn't make him money, but it met such needs of his as nurturing, feeling important, giving, and many others. The strategy quickly produced leads on future (paying) students, and Raphael had three paying students in very little time.

In the end, through a combination of increased income and decreased spending, Raphael had created a plan that he was not only sure would get him to his savings goal in time, but that represented an exciting new routine that would be even more fulfilling than his current one (Figure 4.14). Rather than feeling limiting, the plan energized him.

This is a very simple example of how to create a functional economic plan that reflects your priorities and values. Raphael was able to identify some small adjustments he could make to his financial behaviors by using his resources (roommates who like to cook together) to meet his needs (ease, comfort, social connection, and consistency with his personality).

Now it's your turn. Start with your current Cash Flow. Then look at the needs list and see if you can think of any other expenses that you should list. Once you are sure that your Cash Flow is complete, start to think about your current strategies for meeting your needs. When you look at your own Cash Flow sheet, how much adjustment do you need to make in order to get your needs met without sabotaging your future security? How can you maximize your resources to meet your needs? Are there ways you can increase your income streams by channeling more resources into assets? Are there some ways you can meet your needs directly without involving financial strategies?

Category		Strategy			Strategy		Category
			Income	Expenses			
		Desk Job at					
Land	Job	Wildlife Org	2600	650	Rent	Exercise	Survival
Labor/Capital	Wrestling	Coaching	0	75	Util	Rest	
Labor/Capital	Guitar	Lessons	150	40	Car ($\frac{1}{2}$ parents)	Sex	
Land	—	—	—	250	Food	Shelter	
Capital	$3000 savings	Savings 2% APR	5	0	Phone (parents)	Transportation	
				75	Yoga	Peace	Security
				50	Lunch	Safety	
				225	Bars	Stability	
				100	Restaurants	Acceptance	Emotional
				275	Entertainment	Adventure	
				50	Taxi	Affction	
				200	Buffr	Belonging	
			2750.50	1990		Communication	
			Saving	**765**		Friendship	
			Goal	**$750**		Fun	
			Left to Find	−$15		Intimacy	
						Love	
						Nurturing	Esteem
						(self or others)	
						Appreciation	
						Recognition	
						Respect	
						To Matter	
						Giving	Self-Actualization
						Growth	
						Independence	
						Personal space	
						Self Expression	
						Awareness	Cognitive/Spiritual
						Creativity	
						Discovery	
						Hope	
						Meaning	
						Purpose	
						Understanding	

Current Savings	$3 000
Savings Goal	$12000
Months till goal	12
Monthly Goal	$750

Figure 4.14   Raphael's Personal Economy

The Power of Perspective

When we think of our money in terms of Resources and Needs, some-thing powerful happens. By moving away from the Cash Flow model of budgeting, which looks only at the flow of money and not at its source or purpose, we start to see a new picture emerge in our mind's eye, and this tells a very different story about how money works.

Remember that in a Cash Flow budget, money comes in as income from somewhere external, and it flows back out as expenses. In the Cash Flow model, our mental picture of money leads us to feel that money management is merely about directing the flow of money as it comes into our lives and flows back out. As I've said before, this is a very disempower-ing way to think. When we think instead about how we use our personal resources to create streams of income, and how our expenses serve to meet our deep personal needs, we see a very different story in our mind's eye. From this perspective, you can see that your money comes from you; it comes from your resources being put to use to create something valuable to others. Likewise, the money you spend goes directly to you; it is used to satisfy your personal needs. *You* are the source and the end of your money. You are the creator and the consumer of your finances. Your money comes from you, and it goes to you. You are the one in control.

One of my favorite things in the world is to see the flash of inspira-tion in people's eyes when they make this shift in perspective. I've heard people say they feel a sense of lightness, as if a weight has been lifted from their shoulders. Others talk about feeling powerful and more pos-itive because they can see that their situation is more flexible than they had thought. It is amazing to watch the creativity pour out as people start to brainstorm how they might begin to change some strategies for meeting their needs directly with resources they already have rather than by creating unnecessary financial strategies that result in higher expenses. While worksheets may not be as dynamic as a workshop, you have all the tools here to have a similarly transformational experience.

Keeping Yourself on Track

Once you've devised your new strategies, the hard part is keeping them until they become habits that you don't even have to think about.

Many budgeting experts have strict methods for tracking expenses such as the envelope method, which requires that you take all of your money in cash and divide it into envelopes by spending category. Other people advise that you set all of your bills to be paid automatically through your bank website or online bill-payment features. Here again, the method is a strategy. Order, peace, security, and stability are some of the needs the strategies meet.

There is no one correct strategy for keeping track of your money. They each have pros and cons, and each will appeal differently to different personality types. If you are distrustful of sharing financial information over the Internet, then paying your bills online will not work for you because it will threaten your needs for peace and security. If you are likely to forget when bills are due until you receive a disconnection notice for your electricity, then the envelope system is probably not for you because it doesn't meet your need for ease. In the same way that developing a plan for making and using your money requires you to be realistic about what you actually care about and what motivates you, when you choose a strategy for tracking your cash flow, you need to work within the bounds of who you realistically are. Some of us are willing to sit down and track our every dollar each week. Others of us would rather have our fingernails pulled out.

A large part of choosing which method will work for you may be the amount of financial slack you have. *Slack* refers to the wiggle room between how much you earn and how much is dedicated to basic costs of living. One unhappy truth about money management is that those of us who have the least money have to be the best at managing it. If you have lots of slack, making some emotional purchases or losing track of your spending may not have a huge effect on your situation. People with slack can be less diligent about tracking and make lots of financial mistakes before it becomes a real problem. On the other hand, if you have very little wiggle room, you must be incredibly persistent about keeping track, as a small slip in spending or forgotten payment can have a very large impact on your finances. If you are living paycheck to paycheck, then chances are you need to be very careful with tracking. In this case, the envelope system may be a very good choice for you, because when you deal with cash you will be constantly reminded of how much or how little you have to spend. If, on the other hand, you have plenty of slack in your budget, you may still opt for an envelope system in order to train yourself to be more mindful of where your money goes and give yourself pause from time to time. A cash-only method of tracking your spending can work extremely well for people who are trying to limit spending and gain insight into where, exactly, their money is going. Studies have shown that paying with cash is more painful, on average, than paying with a card, so this method can help some people rein in spending by drawing more attention to the actual transfer of cash taking place each time a purchase happens.

On the other hand, this means that paying bills is more painful as well, which may sabotage the feeling of satisfaction we can derive from the needs we are meeting with those expenses. I've also heard people say that they actually feel more free to spend cash than they do to use a debit card. Once the cash has been taken out of the bank, you know it is available to spend, so handing it over to a sales clerk may be *less* painful in some ways than handing over a card that draws from an account that also pays your bills. Studies of financial behavior measure *trends*, but they don't capture the nuances of our individual differences. You need to know yourself and choose the method that will work for you.

Auto-payment can be a lifesaver for those of us who tend toward financial disorganization. When I first started out on my own, I could hardly be bothered to keep track of when bills were due. My teenage brain was far more concerned with my social life than my finances, and as a result, I rarely looked at my bills until I saw a pink paper indicating a disconnection notice. One year, despite having a tax refund due to me, I neglected to fill out the paperwork because I simply did not want to bother with the form. My hatred of paperwork effectively cost me nearly $1,000 that year. Once I decided to take charge of my financial life, I tried to be more diligent about remembering due dates and writing checks regularly, but after some time I came to accept that I will never enjoy paperwork, and the more I can automate about the bill-paying process, the better. For me, the advent of the online bill-payment service was a godsend. Yes, it took a few hours to gather all of my bills, enter all of the information, schedule when the payments should be sent, and make sure that there would always be enough in my account to cover them, but once that initial administrative work was finished, I was able to rest easy. My bills were paid, and I no longer wasted precious mental energy thinking about them. I stopped incurring late charges for lack of organization, and my credit score slowly and steadily improved.

For people who are learning to get more involved in their financial decisions, yet want to make the process of tracking their money simple, I recommend a kind of hybrid method between the envelope system and automated bill payment. For all of your regular and fixed bills such as your housing payments, utilities, subscriptions, et cetera, go ahead and set up automatic bill payments. These are items that do not require much thought or decision making because they are already set, and the most important aspect of managing this type of budget item is making sure the bills get paid on time. With that in mind, setting up automated payments for your regular bills and fixed expenses can save you time and energy, as well as reduce your cognitive load and financial stress.

When it comes to the items that can vary from time to time such as groceries, bar and restaurant budgets, gifts, fuel and maintenance for your car, veterinarian visits, and other flexible categories, use an envelope system for these. These budget items require more monitoring than your fixed expenses because they can change depending on circumstances and emotions. An envelope system is very simple: Withdraw the total budgeted amount for all of your flexible budget items *in cash* each pay period. Then, divide the cash into separate envelopes for each spending category. Some of these, like vet visits or vehicle maintenance, will slowly grow fatter as time goes on. Then, when you need to buy new tires or take the cat to be neutered, the money will be waiting for you. Others, like the grocery or babysitting envelopes, will be filled and emptied more regularly. With these categories, you may notice yourself tending to overspend in one, and regularly moving money from another to make up the difference. This act of shifting cash between envelopes can be a very useful teacher to you. If you are trying to learn to live within your means, using cash for your flexible finance categories will not only help you stay within your limits, but it will likely help you to gain insight into your emotional states when you are making those decisions. The act of taking cash out of your envelopes, or moving cash between them when one is emptied, serves as a physical reminder of the tradeoffs we make with our money, and our needs. Using cash for your flexible budget items, even just for a few months, can teach you a lot about which needs are the most important to you, and thus how your needs are organized. You may even want to draw your own version of a needs hierarchy that reflects how *your* needs are prioritized, and check your economic plan against that from time to time to make sure you are living in accordance with your own priorities and values.

Regardless of *how* you track your finances, tracking them is essential to financial health. At HelloWallet, one of our consumer finance experts found that people who tracked their money in our system had $150,000 more, on average, than those in their same income and age brackets who did not monitor their budget.[9] In some ways, any type of tracking is better than nothing. However, there is some evidence that the tool you use to track your money may have an effect on your overall financial health down the line. In a recent market research study performed by Morningstar and Capita, we found that people who used *any* method of tracking their finances had higher scores on the Financial Management Behavior Scale. However, only people who used a spreadsheet or financial management software showed significantly better debt management and savings behaviors than their peers. Other methods of tracking, like checking your bank's website or using pen and paper, only seemed to improve day-to-day cash management, and did not have a beneficial impact on other financial management behaviors like reducing debt, investing, or saving for the future. Using a spreadsheet or financial management software requires more effort than other methods of tracking, but it seems to have a real payoff. The trend we saw in our research was that the more involved a person was with tracking their money, the more likely they were to be on track in many other areas of money management. Clearly, there is a huge financial benefit to counting your money.

All of the exercises and stories up to this point were meant to get you ready to do this on your own. This method takes time and a willingness to reflect on yourself, your needs, your values, and your behaviors. It is far more difficult than a simple Cash Flow budget. However, it is well worth the extra time and effort. The few hours you will spend solving the puzzle of how to make your *personal economy* grow and thrive will pay off in better sleep, more satisfied needs, personal pride, and long-term financial stability. If you have done the deep work of thinking through your needs and creating realistic strategies to meet them, you should feel a sense of peace with your plan. If you have the sense that you might fight against any part of it, there is still a need or two that are not satisfied by the plan as it is. Keep working until you feel a sense of peace, pride, and joy with your plan. This is your financial life you are crafting. Make it one you truly love.

Enjoying a Loaded Life: Living in Harmony with Your Money and Your Values

We have come a long way from the Cash Flow budget. The concepts and exercises I have laid out in this book will, with practice, lead to a very different way of interacting with your money. My hope is that it will bring you more peace, stability, freedom, and personal power in your financial life. As well as helping you manage your finances, this method of creating a personal economic plan will, I hope, give you the tools you need to stabilize your financial life so that you are free to pursue your nonmonetary goals. At the same time, I recognize that this way of managing your money requires more thought and work than a simple Cash Flow budget, so why bother to practice it at all? The best answer I can give to that challenge is that, while the numbers on your Cash Flow budget may change with the winds of time and chance, your financial life will always be about how you use your resources to meet your needs. If you think about your money in these big-picture terms, you will be equipped to adapt easily to shifts in your specific economic circumstances. Yes, it takes time and adjustment to learn this way of money management, but it is a technique that puts you at the helm of your financial life, and allows you to keep your eyes on the big picture, even while attending to the nitty-gritty details of daily financial decisions.

Returning to the concepts of psychological distance and construal level, you may recall that when we think about things using low-level construal, we tend to focus on *how* something is done, and when we use high-level construal, we think about *why.* The Cash Flow budget is a low-level view of your finances. It tells you exactly how your money moves from income to expenses and savings. Thinking about resources and Needs is a high-level view. Your personal economy puts it all together. You have the *how* as well as the *why* all in one place. It's the whole picture, and you are the artist.

Taking the time to think through your personal economic plan is an up-front investment of time and mental energy. It certainly takes more time, as well as deeper thought and consideration, than simply listing your income and expenses. Nevertheless, I believe this approach to money management will save you time and stress in the long run. When you learn to take stock of your resources and thoughtfully direct them to serve as many needs as possible, and to minimize the financial strategies you use to meet your needs, you are not only taking charge of your personal finances, but your life satisfaction as well. By using your resources creatively and thoughtfully, and making sure to attend to all of your needs, the LOADED budgeting method promises to help you build a plan that will never leave you feeling deprived or un-happy, because *all* of your needs are satisfied. Budgeting does not need to feel like being on a diet; I believe it should not feel limiting, or you will not stick to it for the long term.

The LOADED method of managing your money is not just a strat-egy for getting your numbers to balance. It is a method for integrating your financial strategies into the bigger picture of your life. Your deepest values express themselves through the needs that are most im-portant to you, and the way you direct your resources should work in harmony with your needs, not against them. Learning strategies for channeling your resources in both financial and nonfinancial ways to directly meet your needs is a deeply satisfying practice. Remember that you are the source of your money. Your resources are yours to manage. Likewise you are the beneficiary of your money. Your expenses all go to serve your personal needs. With time and experience, this way of thinking about your money will become easier, and you will be able to adapt more quickly to changes in your physical circumstances.

I encourage you to continue working with the exercises in this book for some time. Core beliefs take time to change, and our personal narratives can shift depending on our mood or perspective. Training yourself to think further into the future and to picture your future with detail and clarity can also take time, and I recommend doing visualization exercises on a regular basis until your mental timeline is significantly longer. Keeping affirmations of your core values in your wallet is something that takes barely any time, but can help retrain your thoughts in moments of ego depletion. Developing new strategies to meet your needs can also take time, as well as trial and error, until you find solutions that work well for you. All of these activities have the potential to create positive change in your financial life, but none of them will be a silver bullet that changes everything in a moment.

The methods outlined here are intended to bring your sense of financial control inward, to help you take charge of your financial life. They are meant to help you blend the "how" and the "why" of your financial decisions, to empower you to make the most of your personal resources in order to meet all of your needs, and to offer a way of working with your money that feels deeply satisfying and sustainable, even through the twists and turns of life's constant change. The numbers on your cash flow sheet may change from time to time, either through chance or by deliberate action, but *why* you do what you do is not as easily altered by time or circumstance. You will always be directing your resources in service of your fundamental needs. This way of thinking about your finances allows you to be flexible and adapt your strategies while maintaining a lifestyle that is deeply satisfying at every stage.

I wish you all the best in your financial life. It is my sincere hope that the concepts and methods in this book will help you take the necessary steps to make changes in your attitudes and financial behaviors that are both satisfying and sustainable. Money will continue to be one of the most loaded and taboo topics of conversation, but I hope you now have the ability to speak about it to others, and yourself, with different words. You will continue to be surrounded by money messages, but I hope you will hear them now with different, more discerning ears. The future will always be tomorrow, but I hope you can learn to see it with new, and clearer eyes. The rich and the poor will always have differences, but I hope you can judge them both with a newly compassionate heart. Lastly, when it comes to your daily financial decisions, I sincerely hope that you are able to find ways to be deeply satisfied, regardless of how you adjust the numbers on your cash flow sheet. Take heart, you have many resources.

You are loaded.

Notes

1. I am *not* saying that we all have the same opportunities or the same resources. We don't. Anywhere you look you can see examples of privilege and lack. I also do not mean to suggest that anyone can get rich if they just try hard enough. There are real and systemic barriers for many people that won't change without collective, organized action as a society.
2. Center for Nonviolent Communication, "Needs Inventory," 2005, www.cnvc.org/Training/needs-inventory.
3. You can read the entire *Divine Comedy* online at www.gutenberg .org/files/8800/8800-h/8800-h.htm.
4. I recognize that we have a Social Security system in the United States. I challenge anyone to prove to me that most people living solely on Social Security are financially secure and satisfied.
5. Annamaria Lusardi, Daniel J. Schneider, and Peter Tufano, "Financially Fragile Households: Evidence and Implications," *National Bureau of Economic Research*, www.nber.org/papers/w17072.
6. HelloWallet Emergency Savings Calculator, http://hellowallet.com/ emergency-savings/#/calculator/1.

7. Federal Trade Commission, "Section 319 of the Fair and Accurate Credit Transactions Act of 2003: Fifth Interim Federal Trade Commission Report to Congress Concerning the Accuracy of Information in Credit Reports," December 2012, www.ftc.gov/reports/section-319-fair-accurate-credit-transactions-act-2003-fifth-interim-federal-trade.

8. Consumer Finance Protection Bureau, "Where Can I Get My Credit Score?," last modified October 14, 2015, www.consumerfinance.gov/askcfpb/316/where-can-i-get-my-credit-score.html.

9. Jake Spiegel, "HelloWallet Infographic: The Power Of Budgeting," *HelloWallet*, January 21, 2014, http://hrpost.hellowallet.com/retirement/hellowallet-infographic-the-power-of-budgeting/.

Appendix A: Self-Assessments

Write Your Personal Financial Narrative

It's already in you. This exercise is to help you see it clearly by writing it down so that you can make some decisions about how well it has been serving you, and whether or not you need to make some adjustments. The prompts below are just a guide. They can help get you thinking, but don't limit yourself to this. Whatever comes to mind, whatever feels important or meaningful, especially things that trigger strong emotion, are worthy of inspection. Take some time to jot down answers to the questions below using simple keywords or phrases. Then you can refer back to them as you write your narrative.

Who have been the two or three most influential people in your life, financially, and how do/did each of them view money?

If money were a character in your life's story, up to this point would you say it has been a friend or an enemy?

What kinds of money messages did you receive growing up? Did the people around you see money as good or evil, sacred or profane? How did their views influence your own perspective?

What words come to mind to finish the sentence, "Money is. . . ." Or, "In my life, money has been. . . .

What emotions do you most strongly associate with money?
Now, grab some paper or pull up your laptop and using your answers to the questions above, write your financial story in two pages or less.

Define Your Core Beliefs

Once you have your personal narrative written, you can start to hunt for the core beliefs hidden within the story. The questions here can help you get started.

- What themes, if any, emerge as you read your narrative? Do the words "never" or "always" appear anywhere in the story? What do you make of these patterns?

- Do you see money messages in the narrative? What are they?

- If your story were a fable, what would be the moral at the end?

- In your story, has money been a friend or enemy? Is it sacred or profane?

- If your financial story was a movie, would any of the characters be familiar? Is there a Scrooge or a Charlie Bucket? A Cinderella or a Robin Hood? Are there any caricatures in your narrative?

- What is your role in the story with respect to money? Are you the one in control, or does circumstance have the upper hand?

Once you've thought these through, try to distill the message of your financial story down to its main point.

Core beliefs are best expressed in one declarative sentence such as, "Money has always been there for me," or, "Money is a necessary evil."

Write each core belief as one simple sentence:

Financial Management Behavior Scale

Financial Management Behavior Scale

Please rate your behavior regarding the following behaviors *over the past 6 months* by circling the number that corresponds to your answer

	Never	Seldom	Sometimes	Often	Always
1 Comparison-shopped when purchasing a product or service	1	2	3	4	5
2 Paid all your bills on time	1	2	3	4	5
3 Kept a written or electronic record of your monthly expenses	1	2	3	4	5
Stayed within your budget or spending plan	1	2	3	4	5
4 Paid off credit card balances in full each month	1	2	3	4	5
5 Maxed out the limit on one or more credit cards	5	4	3	2	1
6 Made only the minimum payment due on a card or loan	5	4	3	2	1
7 Began or maintained an emergency savings fund	1	2	3	4	5
8 Saved money from each paycheck	1	2	3	4	5
9 Saved for a long-term expense such as a car, home, etc.	1	2	3	4	5
10 Contributed money to a retirement account	1	2	3	4	5
Bought bonds, stock, or mutual funds	1	2	3	4	5

Please rate your behavior regarding insurance *over the past year* by circling the number that corresponds to your answer

	Never	Seldom	Sometimes	Often	Always
Maintained or purchased an adequate health insurance policy	1	2	3	4	5
Maintained or purchased adequate property insurance (home, auto, renter's, etc.)	1	2	3	4	5
Maintained or purchased adequate life insurance	1	2	3	4	5

SCORING

	Your Raw Score	How to get your percentage	Your Percentage
Cash Management (Questions 1-4)		Divide your raw score by 10, then multiply by 100	
Credit Management (Questions 5-7)		Divide your raw score by 15, then multiply by 100	
Savings & Investment (Questions 8-12)		Divide your raw score by 25, then multiply by 100	
Insurance (Questions 13-15)		Divide your raw score by 15, then multiply by 100	
Total Financial Management & Behavior Score		Divide your raw score by 75, then multiply by 100	

Adapted from J. Dew and J. J. Xiao, "The Financial Management Behavior Scale: Development and Validation," Journal of Financial Counseling and Planning 22, no. 1 (2011): 43-60.

Emotions and Money (from HelloWallet's 2014 Pilot Study)

Emotions and Money

In the past 6 months, how often have you experienced the following emotions regarding your finances?

		Almost Never	Seldom	About Half the Time	Often	Almost Constantly	Score
1	Anxiety	1	2	3	4	5	
2	Sadness	1	2	3	4	5	
3	Frustration	1	2	3	4	5	
4	Helplessness	1	2	3	4	5	
5	Pride	1	2	3	4	5	
6	Satisfaction	1	2	3	4	5	
7	Joy	1	2	3	4	5	
8	Peace	1	2	3	4	5	
						TOTAL SCORE:	

SCORING: Add the totals for each question group, and **subtract the top box from the bottom** (see below)

		Almost Never	Seldom	About Half the Time	Often	Almost Constantly	Score
1	Anxiety					5	
2	Sadness	1					11
3	Frustration		2				
4	Helplessness			3			
5	Pride	1					
6	Satisfaction	1					5
7	Joy	1					
8	Peace		2				
					Total: 5 minus 11 =		−6

Mental Imagery

Mental Imagery							SCORING
1. When you think about the future, how far ahead do you tend to think?							Add questions 1 and 2
Less than 1 week	1 month or less	Several Months	About a year	Several years	More than 5 years	10 years or more	**2 to 5**
							Lots of room for improvement. Use the visualization and age progression exercises.
1	2	3	4	5	6	7	**6 to 10**
2. How clear and detailed is your vision of the future?							You could benefit from taking a longer view
Extremely vague and without detail						Extremely clear and detailed	
1	2	3	4	5	6	7	**11 to 14** You're in great shape!
Center of Destiny							**1 to 2** External
3. Which statement do you most agree with?							
1	External forces mostly determine what happens in my life						**3** Neutral
2	I have some control, but external forces play a larger role						
3	My life is an *equal* mix of personal choices and external factors						**4 to 5** Internal
4	I mostly control what happens in my life						
5	I determine my own fate						

Behavior Identification Form

What's Your Construal Level?

Any behavior can be described in many ways. Your task is to choose the identification, a or b, that best describes the behavior for you. Simply place a checkmark next to the option you prefer.

Making a list		**Climbing a tree**	
a	Getting organized*	a	Getting a good view*
b	Writing things down	b	Holding on to branches
Reading		**Filling out a personality test**	
a	Following lines of print	a	Answering questions
b	Gaining knowledge*	b	Revealing what you're like*
Joining the Army		**Toothbrushing**	
a	Helping the Nation's defense*	a	Preventing tooth decay*
b	Signing up	b	Moving a brush around in one's mouth
Washing clothes		**Taking a test**	
a	Removing odors from clothes*	a	Answering questions
b	Putting clothes into the machine	b	Showing one's knowledge*
Picking an apple		**Greeting someone**	
a	Getting something to eat*	a	Saying hello
b	Pulling an apple off a branch	b	Showing friendliness*
Chopping down a tree		**Resisting temptation**	
a	Wielding an axe	a	Saying "no"
b	Getting firewood*	b	Showing moral courage*
Measuring a room for carpeting		**Eating**	
a	Getting ready to remodel*	a	Getting nutrition*
b	Using a yardstick	b	Chewing and swallowing
Cleaning the house		**Growing a garden**	
a	Showing one's cleanliness*	a	Planting seeds
b	Vacuuming the floor	b	Getting fresh vegetables*
Painting a room		**Traveling by car**	
a	Applying brush strokes	a	Following a map
b	Making the room look fresh*	b	Seeing countryside*
Paying the rent		**Having a cavity filled**	
a	Maintaining a place to live*	a	Protecting your teeth*
b	Writing a check	b	Going to the dentist
Caring for houseplants		**Talking to a child**	
a	Watering plants	a	Teaching a child something*
b	Making the room look nice*	b	Using simple words
Locking a door		**Pushing a doorbell**	
a	Putting a key in the lock	a	Moving a finger
b	Securing the house*	b	Seeing if someone's home*
Voting			
a	Influencing the election*		
b	Marking a ballot		

SCORING: Total all answers with an *. The higher the score, the more of a HIGH-level construal you tend to use

Adapted from R. R. Vallacher and D. M. Wegner, "Levels of Personal Agency: Individual Variation in Action Identification," *Journal of Personality and Social Psychology* 57 (1989): 660–671.

How Impulsive Are You?

BRIEF SELF-CONTROL SCALE
How impulsive are you?

How much do the following statements describe you?
Circle the number in each box that corresponds to your answer

	Not at all like me	A little like me	Somewhat like me	Mostly like me	Very much like me
I have a hard time breaking bad habits.	5	4	3	2	1
I am good at resisting temptation.	1	2	3	4	5
I am lazy.	5	4	3	2	1
I say inappropriate things.	5	4	3	2	1
I do certain things that are bad for me, if they are fun.	5	4	3	2	1
I refuse things that are bad for me.	1	2	3	4	5
I wish I had more self-discipline.	5	4	3	2	1
People would say that I have iron self-discipline.	1	2	3	4	5
Pleasure and fun sometimes keep me from getting work done.	5	4	3	2	1
I have trouble concentrating.	5	4	3	2	1
I am able to work effectively toward long-term goals.	1	2	3	4	5
Sometimes I can't stop myself from doing something, even if I know it's wrong.	5	4	3	2	1
I often act without thinking through all the alternatives.	5	4	3	2	1

SCORING: Add up the circled items. Higher totals mean more *self-control*.

Adapted from J. P. Tangney, R. F. Baumeister, and A. L. Boone, "High Self-Control Predicts Good Adjustment, Less Pathology, Better Grades, and Interpersonal Success," *Journal of Personality* 72, no. 2 (2004): 271–324.

Big Five Financial Literacy Questions

Big Five Financial Literacy Questions	A	B	C	D	E
1 Suppose you had $100 in a savings account and the interest rate was 2% per year. After 5 years, how much do you think you would have in the account if you left the money to grow?	More than 102	Exactly 102	Less than 102	Don't Know	
2 Imagine that the interest rate on your savings account was 1% per year and inflation was 2% per year. After 1 year, would you be able to buy more than today, exactly the same as today, or less than today with the money in this account?	More than today	Exactly the same as today	Less than today	Don't Know	
3 Do you think that the following statement is true or false: Buying a single company stock usually provides a safer return than a stock mutual fund?	TRUE	FALSE	Don't Know		
4 A 15-year mortgage typically requires higher monthly payments than a 30-year mortgage but the total interest over the life of the loan will be less.	TRUE	FALSE	Don't Know		
5 If interest rates rise, what will typically happen to bond prices?	They will rise	They will fall	They will stay the same	There is no relationship	Don't Know

Answers: A, C, F, T, B

Explanation

1   Interest in the first year is $2 (2% of the total). In the second year, the interest is $2.04 (2% of 102) and so on. . . .

2   Inflation reduces buying power. If the inflation rate is larger than your savings rate, your buying power drops.

3   A single stock is more volatile than shares of many. Mutual funds are made of many individual stocks, reducing their volatility in comparison to most individual stocks.

4   A 15-year mortgage will require higher payments, but since the balance is paid off sooner, the interest accrued is generally less.

5   Bonds are valued based on a combination of their face value and the interest they earn over time. If the interest rate rises, the face value will generally drop accordingly.

Appendix B: Interventions and Exercises

Most of these exercises are described in the text. This space is for you to jot down notes and responses to ideas that strike you. You will likely want a dedicated notebook for longer written responses.

Change the Narrative

The narrative you wrote (Appendix A) is just one of the millions of stories you might have written about your financial life up to this point. Finding a different way to interpret the events you have experienced can lead to new, more helpful core beliefs. To do this, we have to try to shift our perspective on events that we have seen in one way for a long time. Try the following, and see if you can get a different view:

1. **Are there any other patterns you can see in your story? How would someone with very different views turn your story into a money message?**

2. **How have your core beliefs _helped you_ so far? How have they _hindered_ you?**

3. **Does the person you dream of becoming have the same core beliefs, or different ones?**

4. **Ask a trusted friend to read your narrative.** How do they interpret the meaning of money in your life? What's the moral of the story from their point of view?

Challenging Core Beliefs: Find a Counterexample

Your core beliefs are the result of many years and lots of experience. Changing them is not an easy task, but with some effort, it can be done.

The thing to keep in mind is that if you want to challenge a belief, you need to find a way to prove it wrong so that you won't believe it anymore. You don't have to disprove it completely. You need only to find one case where it is not true, and you can begin to weaken its hold on your mind and behavior. For example, if you have a core belief that money always comes with strings attached, then write down one time that was not true. Just think of one single time that gift of money did not come with expectations or obligations attached to it.

1. Write down one of your core beliefs.

2. Ask yourself, "*Where would I be if I didn't believe this?*" Write your thoughts here.

3. Find one case (anytime throughout the history of the world!) when the statement in your belief was not true.

The next time this belief creeps up, bring the counterexample to mind and remember: It is not *always* true.

Age Progression

Get Comfy With Your Future Self
Age-Progression Exercise*

Age progression software has come a long way in the past few years. You can download free apps for your phone or use one of many free websites. Getting an age-progressed image of your face isn't the hard part of this exercise. The challenge is taking a good, long look.

Quite often when I do this exercise with other people, their first reaction is to laugh and look away. We simply do not like being face to face with the realities of old age and frailty. If the image is printed, people will literally push it away from themselves and look the other way. Our instinct is to distance ourselves from things we don't like, but the purpose of this exercise is to remove that distance and create a feeling of *closeness* between your present self an your future self. If you think the image is unrealistic, try another website, but if it is simply unpalatable, then you're ready to begin the work.

After the shock and the silliness have had their moment, take a deep breath, and look again.

- Do you see the resemblance to your parents and grandparents?
- Can you imagine what it is going to *feel* like when you are this age?
- How do you want to be living then?
- Do you want the person you're looking at to be struggling financially?
- How can you help your inner senior citizen live with dignity?
- What financial decisions can you make now that will help him or her to live gracefully and comfortably?

I highly recommend printing out your picture and placing it somewhere that you will see it several times a day for about a week. Your future self will begin to become real to you, and the consequences of your present actions on their experience will start to feel more important.

---

* Though the hypothesis is yet untested, I have some reason to believe that age progression might have a different effect on people who are natural savers than those who are spenders. This exercise probably works best for spenders who want to give themselves some motivation to save more. If you're already a saver, you might not need this extra push.

Future Visualization Exercises

When I was training to be a personal financial planner, one of the first principles I learned was to start with the end in mind. You can't prepare for a future you haven't thought about. Yes, life will bring unexpected changes to the plan, but that is not a good enough reason not to make one at all. Instead, we need to figure out what we really want, and then we can make a plan that leads in that direction. The specific steps along the way may change, but if you want to live well when you are older, you've got to have a plan. The first step is deciding what you want.

So, take a moment to imagine yourself years from now. Once you have that image, answer the following questions:

Ten years from now. . . .

- How old will you be?
- Where do you *want* to be living (house, apartment, condo, boat, etc.)?
- Will you be in the city, suburbs, or country? Which city? Which country?
- Will anyone be living with you (a spouse, roommate, child, parent)?
- How will you spend your days? Will you be working, traveling, parenting, or puttering? Imagine a day from waking to sleeping. Where do you go? What do you eat? Whom do you see?
- What will be the best part of this life for you? What do you love the most about this imagined future?

Once you've done this, think of one *barrier* to getting there that is *within your control*. What is one thing that you can do, one action you can take, to remove that barrier in the next year?

Exercises to Combat MoneyThink

1. **Write about equality.** This is simple. Just write down three ways that other people are equal to you.

    1.
    2.
    3.

2. **Commune with nature.** Plants! Put them in your office. Put them in your home. Beautiful plants have a unconscious effect that helps us be more generous and trusting. Can't get real nature into your space? Photos of beautiful natural places will do the trick.

3. **Get in touch with awe.** Take a moment and think about a time when you felt a sense of awe. Where were you? What were you doing? How did the experience move you? Write a few sentences about it here.

4. **Train in compassion.** Loving-kindness meditation has actually been shown to change people's brains. If you worry that money might make you mean, then practicing loving-kindness meditation can help. It's very simple. Quiet your mind, relax, and follow these four steps:

    a. First, offer loving-kindness to yourself. Say to yourself, "May I be happy. May I be safe. May I be at ease."
    b. Next, offer loving-kindness to someone you love. A friend, family member, or even a pet. Say to yourself, "May they be happy. May they be safe. May they be at ease."
    c. Then, offer loving-kindness to someone you neither love nor hate; a neutral other. "May they be happy. May they be safe. May they be at ease."
    d. Lastly, and this one is tough, offer loving-kindness to a "difficult other." This should be someone you do not like. It could be an enemy or a person you have conflict with. It can even be someone you don't know but who represents everything you dislike. "May they be happy. May they be safe. May they be at ease."

Practice this often, and your compassion will grow over time.

Affirm Core Values

Reminding yourself of the things that matter most to you can be a huge help when you're experiencing ego-depletion, fatigue, or temptation. Figuring out what your core values are is not always simple. The questions below can help you brainstorm at least a few.

Questions to help you uncover core values:

1. **What qualities do you most admire in others?**

2. **What makes your heart sing?** When you feel great joy, your values are saying, "Thank you." If you love to see random acts of kindness or generosity, you probably value those things very highly. What brings a huge smile to your face?

3. **What makes you angry?** Anger is quite often a response to one of your core values being violated. If you hate it when people interrupt you, you might value patience and respect.

4. **What breaks your heart?** Again, the negative emotional response can be due to a core value. Does it break your heart to see loneliness? You probably value connection very highly.

Once you've listed a few core values, write them as simple, declarative sentences. For example: "I care deeply about being kind to others." Write each one down on a note card or slip of paper, and keep them in your wallet. When you are tempted to spend money emotionally, look them over for a nice boost of positive motivation.

Cash Flow Worksheet

Cash Flow Worksheet

Income	Expenses

—

Savings

Resources Worksheet

Resources Worksheet

Resources	Assets	Income

Total

Expenses and Needs Worksheet

Expenses and Needs Worksheet		
Expenses	**Strategy (Liability)**	**Needs**
		(Category) **Survival**
		Food Exercise Rest Sex Shelter Transportation
		Security
		Order Peace Safety Stability
		Emotional
		Acceptance Adventure Affection Belonging Communication Friendship Fun Intimacy Love Nurturing (self or others)
		Esteem
		Appreciation Recognition Respect To matter
		Self-Actualization
		Giving Growth Independence Personal space Self-expression
		Cognitive/Spiritual
		Awareness Creativity Discovery Hope Meaning Purpose Understanding

Your Personal Economy

Your Personal Economy

Resources | **Strategy (Asset)** | **Income** | **Expenses** | **Strategy (Liability)** | **Needs**

(Category)
Land

Labor

Capital

Needs

| **(Category)** |
| Survival |
| Food |
| Exercise |
| Rest |
| Sex |
| Shelter |
| Transportation |
| **Security** |
| Order |
| Peace |
| Safety |
| Stability |
| **Emotional** |
| Acceptance |
| Adventure |
| Affection |
| Belonging |
| Communication |
| Friendship |
| Fun |
| Intimacy |
| Love |
| Nurturing (self or others) |
| **Esteem** |
| Appreciation |
| Recognition |
| Respect |
| To matter |
| Giving |
| Growth |
| **Self-Actualization** |
| Independence |
| Personal space |
| Self-expression |
| **Cognitive/Spiritual** |
| Awareness |
| Creativity |
| Discovery |
| Hope |
| Meaning |
| Purpose |
| Understanding |

TOTAL

TOTAL

SAVING

Just-In-Time Financial Education Resources

Just-In-Time Financial Education Resources		
Resource	**What You'll Find There**	**URL**
Jump$tart	Lesson plans, printouts, videos, books, and workbooks on financial topics for every age range.	www.jumpstart.org/resource-center-clearinghouse.html
Institute for Financial Literacy	Links to websites on many financial topics for various age groups, as well as a glossary of important financial terms.	https://financiallit.org/resources/resource-lists/
U.S. Treasury	Games for kids, short articles, links and budgeting resources for all ages	www.mymoney.gov
Practical Money Skills	Games, apps, videos, lesson plans, calculators, and articles on many topics of personal finance	www.practicalmoneyskills.com/
Khan Academy	Free courses on a variety of financial topics	https://www.khanacademy.org

About the Author

DR. SARAH NEWCOMB is a behavioral economist at Morningstar, Inc. where she works to integrate behavioral science into financial management applications. Dr. Newcomb holds a PhD in behavioral economics, a master's degree in financial economics, and a master's certification in personal financial planning. Through speaking, writing, and product development, she aims to translate the findings from scholarly research into practical and useful tools for everyone. She lives with her daughter in Washington, DC.

Index

NOTE: Page reference in *italics* refer to figures.